The Language of Jesus
Introducing Aramaic

Stephen Andrew Missick

Stephen Andrew Missick *The Language of Jesus: Introducing Aramaic*

The photograph on the cover of this book is a picture of the Aramaic speaking Christian village of Maloula in Syria and was taken by the author.

Table of Contents

What is Aramaic?

Two thousand years ago a young man proclaimed a message and lived a life that changed the course of history. This man, Jesus of Nazareth, claimed to be the savior promised long before by the ancient prophets of Israel. Still, people are seeking the answer to the question, "Who was Jesus?" For hundreds of years people have been searching for the Jesus of history. Scholars have been shifting through archeological evidence and ancient manuscripts to discover answers. One important avenue of research has been strangely overlooked. The best way to discover the real Jesus and the true meaning behind his words is to investigate those words in the language in which they were first uttered, Aramaic.

The Aramaic language is a Semitic language closely related to Hebrew. It is not Arabic. Aramaic is a distinct Semitic language. While it is very similar to Hebrew it is not a dialect of Hebrew. Aramaic is not Armenian. Armenian and Aramaic are totally different languages. Aramaic came to be an important language of the Jewish people after the tribe of Judah endured the exile in Babylonia that is called 'the Babylonian Captivity'. This period of exile lasted from 586 until 539. During this period the language of many of the common Jewish people switched from Hebrew to Aramaic. The books of Daniel and Ezra are partially written in Aramaic. After the exile Ezra had to interpret the scriptures in

Aramaic so that the people could understand them. (Hebrew did remain a living language in certain circles.)

While promoting his film *The Passion of the Christ* Mel Gibson stated that Aramaic was a "dead language". This movie depicted the final hours of Christ's earthly ministry in such an authentic manner that it was filmed with the actors speaking the original Aramaic. Mel Gibson's comment about Aramaic being a dead language is not true. Aramaic is still spoken by the Assyrian and Chaldean Christians of Iraq. These ancient Christians have preserved for us an important version of the Bible in the Aramaic language. This Aramaic Bible is called the *Peshitta* Bible. The Gospels in the *Peshitta* represent an ancient translation of the Bible back into a form of Aramaic almost identical to Aramaic of Jesus. The *Peshitta* Bible is a valuable tool for studying the words of Jesus in the original Aramaic.

In the late 1800s some scholars began to use these important Aramaic sources to understand Jesus and his teachings better. Two translations of the Aramaic New Testament were made by James Murdock and John Wesley Etheridge respectively. More recently reputable scholars have continued this work. These scholars include C. F. Burney, Joachim Jeremias, Bruce Chilton and Maurice Casey.

In his book *Jesus: Apocalyptic Prophet of the New Millennium* Bart Ehrman brings out these two important points about understanding the Jesus of history. First, we need to understand Jesus as a native of the ancient Middle East and as belonging to it's Semitic culture. Secondly, we need to understand him as a person who thought in and spoke the Aramaic language. Bart Ehrman said, "Jesus was Jewish. Realizing the Jewishness of Jesus is critical is we are to make sense of his teachings. For despite the fact that the religion founded in his name quickly came to be filled with non-Jews...it was founded by a Jewish teacher who taught his Jewish followers about the Jewish God who guided the Jewish people by means of the Jewish Law. Jesus kept and discussed Jewish customs like prayer and fasting, he worshiped in Jewish places of worship like the synagogue and the Temple, and he kept Jewish feasts like the Passover...He maintained that God's will was revealed in the books written by Moses, especially in "the Law" that was delivered to Moses on Mount Sinai...Most of Jesus' teachings, in fact, relate in one way or another to his understanding of Jewish Law. This Jewish Law, of course included the Ten Commandments, but it contained much more besides..."About Aramaic Ehrman says, "there are multiple attested traditions that Jesus spoke Aramaic. Sometimes, for example, the Gospels quote his words directly without translating them into Greek (see Mark 5:41, 7:34; John 1:42). It is also indicated in the Gospels that Jesus could read the scripture in Hebrew (e.g., Luke 4: 16-20; see also Mark 12: 10, 26), and that he eventually became known as an interpreter of them. He is sometimes, for example, called "rabbi," that is, "teacher" (see Mark 9:5; John 3:2)...There are no traditions that specifically indicate that Jesus spoke Greek, although some historians have surmised that living in Galilee where Greek was widely known [among non-Jews], he may have learned some. Moreover, some have suspected that he communicated with Pontius Pilate in Greek at his trial...At best we can say that it is at least possible that Jesus was tri-lingual-that he normally spoke Aramaic, that he could at least read the Hebrew Scriptures, and the he may have been able to communicate a bit in Greek. The final point is, in my judgment, the least assured." Scholarly consensus and data from the New Testament agrees that the primary spoken language of Jesus, the language he used when performing cures and teaching the multitudes, was Aramaic. Alan Millard in *Discoveries from the Time of Jesus* states that, "A Jewish craftsman's son brought up in Nazareth, a town on a main road, could be expected to talk in Aramaic, to use Greek when necessary, and to have more than a reading knowledge of Hebrew."

In Aramaic the name Jesus is pronounced Yeshua. In Galilee this name was pronounced Yeshu and in modern Aramaic it is pronounced closer to the Galilean pronunciation as Eshoo. (Until recently the Jewish people referred to Jesus as Yeshu in the Hebrew language.)The Greek language had no 'Y' or 'sh' sound and many Greek names end with an 's' (due to Greeks declensions) so the Greeks pronounced Yeshua as Iesous, which came into English as 'Jesus'. In this book in order to facilitate comprehension I will most often use the English form, Jesus. In his native Aramaic Jesus would have been known as Yeshua Bar Youseff Men Nasrath, "Jesus son of Joseph from Nazareth".

In my Aramaic work I have encountered opposition and even anger and hostility at my contention that Aramaic was the primary language of Jesus. Certain 'Messianic Jews' (Jewish people who believe that Jesus is the Messiah) claim that Jesus spoke only Hebrew. Students of New Testament Greek will claim that Jesus spoke in Greek since the New Testament is written in Greek. Dr. Spiro Zodhiates, a recognized scholar of the Greek New Testament whom I have had the pleasure to meet, conceded that Jesus preached his sermons in Aramaic rather than Greek. (I recognize the Greek text of the New Testament as the authoritative word of God. Looking at the Aramaic words behind the Greek deepens our understanding of what Jesus actually said.) It should be remembered that the Old Testament was composed and is written in both Hebrew and Aramaic. The importance of Aramaic is also illustrated in that it is blessed in the Talmud. (The Talmud is a collection of Rabbinic commentaries on the Sacred Scriptures. The Talmud are authoritative texts for modern Judaism. The Talmud are written both in Hebrew and Aramaic. One Aramaic section is called the

Gemara, which is the Aramaic word for completion.) The Rabbinic Blessing of Aramaic says,

> "Let not Aramaic be lightly esteemed by thee, seeing that the Holy One (Blessed Be He) hath given it honor in the Law, the Prophets and the Writings"
> Palestinian: Tractate Sata 7:2

This means that all three sections of the Hebrew divisions of the Old Testament contain a portion in Aramaic. (The Rabbis divide the books of the Old Testament into different sections than Christians do. These sections are called the Torah (the Law), the Kithiavin (the Writings), and the Nebiyiem (the Prophets). Aramaic in the Tanakh (The Old Testament) includes the following sections: The Law, Genesis 31:47, The Writings, Daniel 2:4-7:28, Era 4:6-8 and 7:12-26, and The Prophets, Jeremiah 10:11 (2 Kings 18:17)

The first use of Aramaic in the Old Testament is in Genesis 31:46 when Laban and Jacob made the covenant, "May the Lord watch between you and me when we are absent one from another". The place where this covenant was made was called Jegar Sahadutha ('Heap of Witness' in Aramaic) by Laban and Galeed ('Heap of Witness' in Hebrew) by Jacob. Laban the Syrian (or Aramean) speaks in Aramaic and Jacob the Israelite speaks in Hebrew (or Canaanite). Linguists classify

9

Hebrew as a form of Canaanite and as a dialect of the language spoken by the Phoenicians and Carthaginians. The language we call Hebrew is called 'the Jews language' (Judean) and 'the lip of Canaan' (Canaanite) in the Bible (Isaiah 36:11, Isaiah 19:18). While Aramaic words are interspersed throughout the Old Testament several chapters of Daniel and Ezra are written in Aramaic rather than Hebrew.

I attended a seminar in which Mel Gibson was mocked for depicting Aramaic rather than Hebrew as the language of Jesus. ("What does "Mad Max" know?," the speaker asked.) Mel Gibson in using Aramaic showed that he seriously studied the most ancient sources and this use of Aramaic was an informed decision that reflects scholarly consensus. This scholarly consensus is based on data from the New Testament, ancient sources and archeological discoveries.

Joachim Jeremias stated in his *New Testament Theology*, "The mother-tongue of Jesus was a Galilean version of western Aramaic. We find the nearest linguistic analogies to the sayings of Jesus in the popular Aramaic passages of the Palestinian Talmud and Midrashim which have their home in Galilee…In addition to the sentences and words preserved in the original Aramaic [in the New Testament], there are many passages in which an underlying Aramaic wording can be disclosed. This includes expressions which are idiomatic in Aramaic but alien to both Hebrew and Greek

(Aramaisms), and translation mistakes which show up when recourse is had to Aramaic."

Maurice Casey in *Aramaic Sources of Mark's Gospel* says, "The Gospel of Mark is written in Greek, though Jesus spoke Aramaic…It follows that the change in language from Aramaic to Greek was part of a cultural shift from a Jewish to a Gentile environment. If therefore we wish to recover the Jesus of history, we must see whether we can reconstruct his sayings, and the earliest accounts of his doings, in their original Aramaic. This should help us to understand him within his own cultural background."

Joseph A. Fitzmyer in *The Semitic Background of the New Testament* says, "As for the language that Jesus would have used, the evidence seems to point mainly to Aramaic…Jesus used Hebrew on occasion…the consensus of opinion at the moment seems to support Aramaic as the language commonly used by Jesus and his immediate disciples in Palestine."

In *Our Translated Gospels* Charles Cutler Torrey concluded, "The material of our Four Gospels is all Palestinian in which it was originally written is Aramaic, then the principle language of the land; with the exception of the first two chapters of Luke which were composed in Hebrew."

Gustaf Dalman in *The Words of Jesus: Considered in the Light of Post-Biblical Jewish Writings and the Aramaic Language* states that , "From all these considerations must be drawn the conclusion that Jesus grew up speaking the Aramaic tongue, and that He would be obliged to speak Aramaic to His disciples and to the people in order to be understood."

Matthew Black in *An Aramaic Approach to the Gospels and Acts* says, "Jesus must have conversed in the Galilean dialect of Aramaic, and His teaching was probably almost entirely in Aramaic."

According to Biblical archeologist John Romer in *Testament: The Bible and History*, "Recent linguistic analysis of all four gospels, however, has tied them not to these grand cities of the Empire, but to the verbal culture of Palestine itself. The construction of their Greek texts, the shading and coloring of the writing strongly suggest that much of them had been translated from Palestinian Aramaic, Jesus' own language."

The New Covenant: Newly Translated from the Greek and Informed by Semitic Sources by Willis Barnstone contains the following interesting quote,

> ...he [Jesus] spoke to his followers and other wayfarers in Aramaic, and except for a few phrases scattered throughout the Gospels, none of his Aramaic sayings have survived. I have wondered for some time how this could be, and wondered even more that Christian scholars have never joined in my wonder. If you believe in the divinity of

Jesus, would you not wish to have preserved the actual Aramaic sayings themselves? Were they lost, still to be found in a cave somewhere in Israel?...For some years now. I have asked these questions whenever I have met a New Testament scholar, and I have met only blankness. *Yet surely this puzzle matters. Aramaic and Greek are very different languages, and the nuances of spirituality and wisdom do not translate readily from one into the other. Any sayings of Jesus, open or hidden, need to be regarded in this context...*

The New Testament indicates that Aramaic was the language Jesus spoke. When Jesus was on Golgotha (Aramaic for "Skull place") he cried out, in Aramaic, "Eloi, Eloi Lama Sabachtani!" Which means "My God, My God, why have you forsaken me?" in Aramaic-not Hebrew. (See Mark 15:34). Had Jesus been speaking Hebrew, he would have said, "Eli, Eli lama azabtani."

The disciples have Aramaic names such as Thomas, which is Aramaic for "Twin, " Martha, which is Aramaic for "Lady" and Cephas, which is Aramaic for "Stone." Scholarly consensus is that Aramaic was the language of Jesus. John P. Meier in "A Marginal Jew: Rethinking the Historical Jesus" stated, "The question of the language(s) Jesus spoke is a complex one, mirroring the complex situation of 1st century Palestine as a "quadrilingual" country.

There is no reason to believe that Jesus knew or used Latin, the language employed almost exclusively by the Roman conquerors. It is likely that he knew and used some Greek for business purposes or general communication with Gentiles, including perhaps Pilate at his trial. But neither his occupation as a woodworker in Nazareth nor his Galilean itinerary, restricted to strongly Jewish towns and villages, would demand fluency in and regular use of Greek. There is thus no reason to think that Jesus regularly taught the crowds who flocked to him in Greek. As for Hebrew, Jesus would have learned it in the Nazareth synagogue or a nearby school, and he probably used it at times when debating Scripture with Pharisees or scribes. Yet, as a teacher who directed himself to the mass or ordinary Jewish peasants, whose everyday language was Aramaic, some traces of which remain embedded in the text of our Greek Gospels. To be more precise, Jeremias identified Jesus' Aramaic as a Galilean version of western Aramaic, distinct in some words and usages from the Aramaic spoken in Judea. Matthew's version of Peter's denial may be alluding to such differenced when the bystanders say to Peter: "Truly you also belong to them [the followers of Jesus *the Galilean*], for ever your speech betrays you" (Matthew 26:73)…Indeed, the very existence of Aramaic targums (translations) of the Hebrew Scriptures argues that a good number of ordinary Jews present in the synagogue could not understand Hebrew even when it was spoken, to say nothing of an ability to read or write it."

I believe that the life of Jesus is the most momentous event in history. As such we must be careful to properly understand the historical context of the life of Jesus. We mustn't idealize the period but carefully use the text of the New Testament and other historical and archeological evidences to glean historical facts. Using biblical and scientific methodology, historians have determined that Aramaic was the language of Jesus Christ. But the question remains, "Did Jesus ever speak Hebrew?" Jesus probably did read Hebrew and used it when reading from or expounding scriptures. He also would have recited certain prayers (such as the Amidah) in Hebrew. Joachim Jeremias believed that Jesus would have almost exclusively spoken Aramaic but he concedes that Jesus probably kept the Passover service, especially during the Last Supper, in Hebrew rather than Aramaic.

Flavius Josephus was a Jewish historian who wrote his monumental *The Jewish War* and *The Antiquities of the Jews* during the time that the New Testament was being written. Josephus was a Jew born in the Holy Land. He wrote *The Jewish War* in what he called his 'ancestral language' and then re-wrote it in Greek. So what was his ancestral language? Josephus said he wrote initially in his ancestral language for two reasons. The first is, as a Jew from the Holy Land he did not have a command of the Greek language. He says,

15

I have also taken a great deal of pains to obtain the learning of the Greek; although I have so accustomed myself to speak our own tongue, I cannot pronounce Greek with sufficient exactness. For my nation does not encourage those that learn the languages of many nations. On this account, as there have been many who have done their endeavors, with great patience, to obtain this Greek learning, there have yet hardly been two or three that have succeeded therein, who were immediately rewarded for their pains.

This means that very few Jews that lived in the Holy Land could speak Greek or speak it well. The second reason was that Josephus was hoping that the version of his book written in his native tongue could be read by gentiles in Assyria, Chaldea and Babylonia, since his native tongue was their native tongue as well. In the first century this region was Aramaic speaking and the direct descendents of the Assyrians, Chaldeans and Babylonians still speak Aramaic till this day. (The writings of Josephus in Aramaic were preserved in Aramaic by Aramaic Christians who looked upon them as important sacred writings.) This proves that Aramaic was the ancestral language of the common Jew born in the Holy Land during the first century.

In Mark 5:41 Jesus resurrects the daughter of Jairus, the ruler of the synagogue, by uttering,

"Talitha, Qumi". This is good basic Aramaic. "Talya" is Aramaic for 'little boy'. "Talitha" is Aramaic for 'little girl'. The word "Qum" means 'to rise' or 'get up'. I have actually heard someone claim that Jesus was referring in Hebrew to a 'tallit' or Jewish prayer shawl and was not speaking in Aramaic. No reputable scholar would say this. Mark, under the inspiration of the Holy Spirit, accurately translates this Aramaic passage as meaning "Little Girl, Arise". I have seen no evidence of Jesus or Jews of the first century using such prayer shawls. Paul says that use of such head covering is dishonorable (1 Corinthians 11: 4 and 7). Paul also said that the Jewish Christian community in Jerusalem had no such custom of using prayer shawls (1 Corinthians 11:16). (There is no historical or archeological evidence that Jews used prayer shawls at the time of Christ.) On the other hand Jesus did indeed wear the tassels on the edge of his garment that were commanded by the Law of Moses (Numbers 15: 37-41, Deuteronomy 22:12). These tassels are mentioned in the Gospel accounts and many people experienced miraculous healings from merely touching the tassels that Jesus wore (Matthew 9:20, 14:36). These tassels are called *tzitzit*. Many Jewish customs originated several centuries after the time of Christ and have no foundation in the biblical era. Jesus was an observant Jew but not of Rabbinic Judaism. Rabbinic Judaism was founded around 200 AD in Galilee. Neither Jesus nor the early Church in

17

Jerusalem used prayer shawls and I have seen no evidence that they were used by Jews at this period either. Use of such devices is actually discouraged in the New Testament. Both proponents of Hebrew and proponents of Greek state that Jesus only spoke Aramaic on rare occasions and that the resurrection of the daughter of Jairus was one such occasion. I read a commentary that stated "Jesus here speaks to the girl in her Aramaic language". This insinuates that Aramaic wasn't Christ's language. These advocates of Greek or Hebrew "primacy" usually concede that certain people in Palestine may have spoken Aramaic but it wasn't the language of Jesus or of the common people. Certain Messianic Jews will say that devout Jews spoke Hebrew. Could you get more devout than to be a ruler of a synagogue? The household of Jairus was Aramaic speaking as were all typical Jewish households. Jesus also grew up in an Aramaic speaking household.

Aramaic is a treasure trove to be mined for deeper understanding of the words of Jesus. The study of Aramaic must be based on the scientific method and research. There are many reputable scholars who have carefully studied Aramaic using sound scholarship that is based on research and the scientific disciplines of history, linguistics and archeology. Aramaic scholars must be careful researchers and knowledgeable of Aramaic literature which includes sections of the Old Testament, the Dead Sea Scrolls, the Targums, the Peshitta, Christian Syriac Aramaic writings and

18

many other writings as well. I admire the work of Joachim Jeremias. Jeremias used the Aramaic language to understand the life and teaching of Jesus in a fuller and more complete way. Jeremais was also familiar with Jewish customs from the first century and with Aramaic and Hebrew literature. While I do not agree with some of Maurice Casey's conclusions (such as his low regard for the Gospel of John and his, in my view, misunderstanding of the Aramaic term 'Son of Man') I admire his scholarly and scientific approach to Aramaic studies. There are certain charlatans in the field of Aramaic studies who use Aramaic to promote heretical ideas and to further the New Age movement. These people are usually Unitarians. Unitarians deny central tenants of Christianity such as the exclusive claims of Jesus Christ, his divinity, the Holy Trinity, the Virgin Birth, the atonement on the cross, the resurrection, the authority of scripture and other central doctrines that were taught by our Lord and Savior Jesus Christ and by his holy apostles. I believe in Christian orthodoxy. Orthodoxy refers to Christian dogma that is based on the writings of the New Testament and the teachings of the apostles. Aramaic is a legitimate field of biblical studies that has been neglected for far too long. I have lived and worshiped among Aramaic Christians. The form of Christianity practiced by the Assyrians and Chaldeans is in no way deviant or cultic. They hold to the same core doctrines all Christians do.

Jesus spoke Aramaic. The life of Jesus is the most important life ever lived. The words of Jesus are the most important words ever spoken. The Good News was a spoken message. It was passed on orally for several years before being confined to writing. The Message of the Kingdom of God was transmitted through language. To understand the mysteries of the kingdom were need to investigate the words as they were spoken by the Lord Jesus and the best way to do this is to look at the words in the Aramaic forms in which they were first uttered

The Biblical and Historical Evidence for Aramaic as the Language of Jesus

Evidence from the Bible

PRAYERS AND TITLES OF DIVINITY

In the New Testament we have Jesus and the early church praying in Aramaic:

Abba, Father

And he said, Abba, Father, all things are possible to thee; take away this cup from me: nevertheless not what I will, but what thou wilt. (Mark 14:36)

The Aramaic word "Abba" is also found in the writings of Paul in Romans 8:15 and Galatians 4:6) Abba is an Aramaic loan word in Modern Hebrew. The Hebrew word is "avi." God is called "Father" over 100 times in the Gospels!

Eloi, Eloi lama sabachtani

And at the ninth hour, Jesus shouted in a loud voice, "Eloi, Eloi lema sabachtani?" which is translated, "My God, my God, for what have you forsaken me?" (Mark 15:34) See also Matthew 27:46.

It Jesus had been speaking Hebrew he would have said, "Eli, Eli, lama azabanti." Jesus is quoting Psalm 22:1 from the Aramaic version. An Aramaic translation (or paraphrase) of the Old Testament is called a Targum. In the Traditional Hebrew text of Psalm 22 it says "Like a lion my hands and feet" but recent archeological discoveries have shown the original reading to be "They have pierced by hands and feet."

Maranatha

"Maranatha" 1 Corinthians 16:22. This word is also used in the Didache. It means "Come, Our Lord." The word for "Lord" in Hebrew is "Adonai."

In Aramaic "Mar" means "Lord." "Maran" means "Our Lord." Maranatha can be translated as either, "Our Lord, Come" (Marana tha) or "Our Lord has come" (Maran atha). Those who argue that Jesus spoke only Hebrew admit that Maranatha is indeed Aramaic but then state that when Paul uses it he "is writing to his non-Israelite, non-Hebrew-speaking audience." But Corinth is between Athens and Sparta! This was a Greek and not an Aramaic-speaking region. Paul uses the "Maranatha" prayer because it is a prayer of the Aramaic speaking mother-church in Jerusalem. The Maranatha prayer has greater significance than just a prophetic significance. Ben Witherington III notes the importance of the Maranatha prayer in his *book The*

Brother of Jesus, "In concluding his letter, Paul, in 1 Corinthians 16:22 offers up a prayer in Aramaic, "Maranatha", which means "Come, Lord." In other words, Jesus is already called Lord by Aramaic speaking Jewish-Christians, and he is prayed to. Now, early Jews did not pray to people who were merely revered dead rabbis, teachers, or even prophets. They might well pray for a rabbi to be raised on the last day, but they would not pray to him and implore him to come. Yet, that is what Paul is doing here, and he is probably echoing a prayer he heard offered in the Jerusalem church, where such prayers were spoken in Aramaic. The dramatic importance of such a prayer should not be underestimated. Jews were forbidden to pray to someone other than God. This prayer strongly suggests that Jesus was included within the earliest Aramaic Jewish Christians understanding of God. In other words, Jesus was already viewed very early on as divine by his earliest followers, and this included James [the Just]. The notion that seeing Jesus as a divine figure was added only late in the first century and was done so only by Gentiles is simply not true."

Son of Man (Barnasha)

The Aramaic phrase "Son of Man" can mean "a man," "a human being," "a person" or even "I" or "me." In the Gospels and other places in the New Testament it is used as a Messianic title. It seems to have come from a prophecy of the coming of a pre-existence divine being in the Aramaic section of the Book of Daniel. Here is an example of one of the prophesies concerning the Son of Man found in the Book of Enoch.

> At that hour, that Son of Man was given a name, in the presence of the Lord of the Spirits, the Before-time, even before the creation of the sun and the moon, before the creation of the stars, he was given a name in the presence of the Lord of the Spirits. He will become a staff for the righteous ones in order that they may lean on him and not fall. He is the light of the gentiles and he will become the hope of those who are sick in their hearts. All those who dwell upon the earth shall fall and worship before him; they shall glorify, bless, and sing the name of the Lord of the Spirits. For this purpose he became the Chosen One; he was concealed in the presence of the Lord of Spirits prior to the creation of the world, and for eternity. And he has revealed the preserved portion of the righteous because they have hated and despised this world of oppression together with all its ways of life and habits in the name of the Lord of Spirits; and because they will be saved in his name and it is his good pleasure that they have life. In those days, the kings of the earth and the

mighty...shall fall on their faces; and they shall not rise up again, nor anyone be found who will take them with his hands and raise them up. For they have denied the Lord of the Spirits and his Messiah.

The Book of Enoch, which was also written in Aramaic, also contains prophecies of the coming of a Messianic figure whom it also calls the Son of Man. The title "Son of Man" which is derived from the Aramaic term "Bar Nasha" is used in all four gospels and in the Acts of the Apostles and the Book of Revelation. (The Epistle of Jude in the New Testament contains a direct quotation from the Book of Enoch.)

Rabboni

Jesus saith unto her, Mary, She turned herself, and saith unto him, Rabbouni; which is to say, Master. (John 20:16)

So Jesus answered and said unto him, "What do you want Me to do for you?" The blind man said to Him, "Rabboni, that I may receive my sight" (Mark 10:51, NKJV)

The Rabbinic title "Rabban" is of Aramaic origin and "Rabbi" is as well.

(NOTE: Hebrew and Aramaic are so similar that some words are the same in both languages also certain words originating from Hebrew, such as HOSANNA, made their way into the Aramaic language. (Hosanna means "Save Now" in Hebrew but came to mean "praise" in Aramaic.) The Aramaic form of the word for Passover, which is "Pascha," is used in the Greek of the New Testament (1 Corinthians 5:7 and many other places). The holiday Hannakah is Aramaic for "Dedication" Jesus celebrated this holiday (John 10:22). Chanukah celebrated the victory of Judah Maccabeus over the Greek oppressors of the Jewish people. Judas Maccabee is Aramaic for "Judah the Hammer." Titles of religious groups such as the Pharisees, from the Aramaic "Separated Ones" and the Essenes, from the Aramaic Chasya, the "Pious" are from Aramaic.

PERSONAL NAMES

Many of the names of people in the New Testament are Aramaic names. Many people in the New Testament have the Aramaic word "bar" in their names. Why would so many people have Aramaic names unless they are speaking Aramaic? Bar is Aramaic for "Son of" while Ben is Hebrew for "Son of." (The "Hebrew only" sect tries to dismiss the fact that there are so many Aramaic names in the New Testament. This demonstrates an error in their methodology- explaining away evidence instead of explaining the evidence.)

Cephas

Jesus looked at him and said, "You are Simon son of John. You will be called Cephas" (which, when translated, is Peter). NIV footnote: Both *Cephas* (Aramaic) and *Peter* (Greek) mean rock. John 1:42. (See also 1 Corinthians 1:12 and Galatians 2:9). In Matthew it is mentioned that when Peter was in the courtyard of the high priest, the people said that he must be a Galilean because "his speech" gave him away. The bystanders were probably commenting of Peter's Galilean accent. The Talmud describes how the Galileans had their own accent to their Aramaic. They didn't pronounced their gutturals clearly. This is probably why Jesus' name in Aramaic is pronounced "Yeshu" in ancient Jewish sources and by Aramaic Christian till this day. "Yeshu" was the Hebrew way of saying "Jesus" until recently, when missionaries introduced the form "Yeshua" into Modern Hebrew.)

Thomas

Simon Peter, Thomas called Twin, Nathaniel of Cana in Galilee, the sons of Zebedee, and two other of his disciples were gathered together. (John 21:2)

In Aramaic Thomas (*teoma*) means "the twin."

27

Simon Canaanean

Canaanean means Zealot, which means "terrorist" or "insurgent." (Mark 3:18)

Mary Magdalene

"And also some women who had been cured of evil spirits and diseases: Mary (called Magdalene) out of whom seven demons had some out; Joanna the wife of Chuza, the manager of Herod's household; Susanna; and many others. (Luke 7: 2-3 NIV) Magdala is the Aramaic word for "tower." Jerome commented that perhaps she acquired this title since her faith was like a tower. However, it seems she is called Mary of Magdala because she came from the town of Magdala.)

Thaddeus and Lebbeus

(Matthew 10:3) Thaddeus means "breast" or "nipple" and Lebbeus, or Libba, means "heart."

Tabitha

In Joppa, there was a disciple named Tabitha, which is translated Dorcas. (Acts 9:36). This Aramaic name means Gazelle.

Martha

Martha in Aramaic means "Lady" (Luke 10:38-41. John 11:1-39, John 12:2).

Bartholomew

Matthew 10:3. Son of Ptolomey or perhaps "son of furrows" or "son of the ploughman."
In Hebrew "Son of…" is Ben. In Aramaic it is "Bar." There are many people with this Aramaic name-form in the New Testament.

Jesus Barabbas

Barabbas means "Son of the Father," He was the one whom was chosen by the crowds to be released instead of Jesus the Messiah. He was a brigand and a murderer (Matthew 27:16)

Simon Bar-Jonas

And Jesus answering, said to him: Blessed art thou Simon Bar-Jona; because flesh and blood hath not revealed it to thee, but my Father who is in heaven. (Matthew 16:17)

Bar-Jonas, means "Son of Jonah." Certain manuscripts read "Son of John" instead. The name "John" was Johannan.

Joseph Barsabbas

Barsabbas was considered as a candidate to be numbered among the Twelve Apostles (Acts 1:23). His name means "Son of the Sabbath," perhaps because he was born on a Sabbath day.

Elymas Bar-Jesus

And when they had gone through the whole island, as far as Pahpos, they found a certain man, a magician, a false prophet, a Jew, whose name was Bar-Jesus. (Acts 12:6)

This man's name means "the Son of Jesus." During the first century, Jesus was a very common name. In his writings, Josephus mentions several different people named "Jesus." The name "Jesus" is a form of the name "Joshua."

Judas Barsabbas

This Barsabas was sent to Antioch carrying a letter from the apostles in Jerusalem (Acts 15: 22). He was a prophet (Acts 15:32) Judas Barsabbas is most likely a close relative of Joseph Barsabbas, possibly his brother.

Joseph Barnabas

Joseph Barnabas (Acts 4:36) from Bar-Nava meaning "Son of Prophecy," translated as "The Son of Encouragement" or "The Son of Consolation." This was the traveling missionary companion of Saint Paul.

NAMES OF PLACES

Gabbatha

"When Pilate heard this, he brought Jesus out and sat down on the judge's seat at a place known as the Stone Pavement (which in Aramaic is Gabbatha)" (John 19: 13).

Josephus in *The Jewish War V. ii. 1:51* states that Gabbatha means "high place' or "elevated place."

Golgotha

"Carrying his own cross, he went out to the place of the Skull (which in Aramaic is called Golgotha.) Here they crucified him, and with him two others-one on each side and Jesus in the middle" (John 19: 17-18). See also Mark 15:22.

Bethany

John 11:1
Meaning "House of Dates"

Bethzatha

John 5:1-15
Jesus performed a miracle at the Pool of Bethzatha. This Aramaic place name is mentioned in the famous Copper Scroll found among the Dead Sea Scrolls. The Copper Scroll is an ancient treasure map from the first century.

Gehenna

Have no fear of those who kill the body, but can by no means kill the soul. Fear him instead who can destroy both soul and body in Gehenna. (Matthew 10:28)

The word "Gehenna" in Aramaic came to be the word used for "the burning hell" or "hell-fire." This was from the symbolism found in the burning rubbish dumps of Gey-Hennom, in the valley outside of Jerusalem. The Aramaic word Gehenna is derived from the Hebrew "Gey-Hennom," meaning "Valley of the Sons of Hennom." This cursed place was a place of idolatrous worship and human sacrifice in the Old Testament era. The Aramaic word "Gehenna" is found in many places in the Greek text of the New Testament but is usually translated as 'hell" in English versions. Also, in should be noted that Jesus in this saying in Matthew 10:28 uses what the Aramaic scholar Joachim Jeremias called the "divine passive." This was reverencing the name of God by speaking of the Lord by means of circumlocutions. The Jewish people at the time of Jesus' ministry would avoid speaking the proper name of God, which is "Jehovah" or "Yahweh." (Actually the original pronunciation wore likely Yahwoh and alternately Yahoo. The Divine Name could also have been originally pronounced "Yahuwoh." The form Yahoo is found in many ancient writings and inscriptions including the ancient Aramaic scrolls used by the Jewish community in Elephantine, Egypt shortly after the time of Ezra and Nehemiah.) Often they would substitute "Name," "Glory," "Heaven" and many other words for the Divine Name. Jesus often uses the "divine passive" when he speaks of God as "Him," "He who" and etcetera.

ARAMAIC WORDS AND PHRASES USED IN THE NEW TESTAMENT

Ephphatha

And looking up to heaven, he sighed and said to him, "Ephphatha," which is "Be opened." (Mark 7:34). This word is Ethpatach and is the same in both Hebrew and Aramaic because these languages are so closely related.

Talitha Koum

And taking the hand of the child, he said to her, "Talitha koum," which is translated, "Little girl, I say to you, get up." (Mark 5:41)

This Aramaic phrase here is important because Jesus is using it in an Aramaic speaking household. So we see that the household of a president of the synagogue is an Aramaic-speaking household. Thus we see that it wasn't just the uneducated who spoke Aramaic but also the educated and the elite. Talitha means little girl-not "Tallit" (garment) nor "Little lamb."

Raca

But I say unto you, that whosoever is angry with his brother without a cause shall be in danger of judgment: and whosoever shall say to his brother, Raca, shall be in danger of the council: but whosoever shall say, Thou fool, shall be in danger of hell fire. (Matthew 5:22)

In the Aramaic of the Talmud, Raka means empty one, fool, empty-headed.

Mammon

No man can serve two masters; for either he will hate the one, and love the other; or else he will hold to the one, and despise the other. Ye cannot serve God and mammon. (Matthew 6:24)

See also Luke 16:9-13 and 2 Clement 6.

This corresponds with how the word the Aramaic word KOWBAIN (debt) is used in the Lord's Prayer. In Christ's teachings, especially in his parables, we see a link between sin and debts and the idea of forgiveness of sins as forgiveness of debt.

Korban

"But you say, "If a man says to his father or his mother, "Whatever profit you might have received from me is Corban"-(that is a gift to God)…" (Mark 7:9-13).

This word refers to an offering or a sacrifice. Modern Assyrians call their Holy Communion service the Korban. In this passage Jesus was condemning a doctrine of the scribes and Pharisees that stated is you swore to give money to them, this released you from the obligation of using that money to support your needy elderly parents. Korban is both Hebrew and Aramaic. "KORBAN" meaning "a gift to God" has been found being used in an Aramaic inscription on an ossuary discovered in Israel.

Evidence from Archeology

The Elephantine Papyri

These Aramaic scrolls are from a Jewish colony in southern Egypt. They date to around 400 BC. They contain legal archives and correspondence to the priesthood in Jerusalem. The letters to Jerusalem were not Hebrew but are Aramaic. These ancient archives show that the post-exilic Jewish community in the Holy Land used Aramaic. They were written in Aramaic, which had become the everyday language of the Hebrew people. Jesus was a post-exilic Jew and lived in an era when Aramaic had largely displaced Hebrew as the language of the Jewish people.

The King Uzziah Tablet

King Uzziah is mentioned in Isaiah 6, 2 Chronicles 26. The Tablet is dates to the first century (the time of Jesus) and says in Aramaic "Herein are the bones of Uzziah, King of the Jews. Do not remove." Sometime during the life of Jesus, the bones of Uzziah the King were exhumed for some unknown reason and re-interred. It is only logical that such an important notice would be written in the most commonly used language so that it could be understood by the greatest number of people.

The Dead Sea Scrolls

"The Dead Sea Scroll Bible" mentions some interesting information about the Dead Sea Scrolls "Song of Solomon" which "features several scribal errors and, although written in Hebrew, contains several Aramaic word forms that reveal Aramaic influence on the scribe" (612).

The majority of the Dead Sea Scrolls are in Hebrew. Many others are in Aramaic (about 20 percent of them) and a few are in Greek.

Why would a scribal community that viewed Hebrew as a holy language use Aramaic at all unless it was the language of the common people? Why would their scribal errors betray an Aramaic influence unless Aramaic was their first language? Their rules for their community and some of their commentary on Scripture are in Hebrew but much of the popular literature such as the Genesis Apocryphon, Enoch and Tobit are in Aramaic. A Targum, Aramaic translation, of Job was discovered. The Testament of Levi, the New Jerusalem and other Aramaic books were discovered among the Dead Sea Scrolls. The Dead Sea Scrolls prove Jewish people in the Holy Land at the time of Jesus' public ministry were Aramaic speakers!

Certain Hebrew Primacists say that Joachim Jeremias and Matthew Black, two respected scholars who investigated Aramaic as the language of Jesus, maintained that Jesus spoke Aramaic because they formed their opinions before the discovery of the Dead Sea Scrolls. However, this is untrue, they were aware of the Dead Sea Scrolls and used them in their research. (Both Black and Jeremias constantly cite the Dead Sea Scrolls in their writings. The many Aramaic scrolls found among the Dead Sea Scrolls were particularly helpful to them. Black and Jeremias show familiarity with a very wide range of ancient Jewish writings.) Actually, the Dead Sea Scrolls are very helpful in reconstructing the words of Jesus in Aramaic since several of them are in Aramaic and Maurice Casey has used them for this purpose.

The Bar Kokhba letters

Bar Kokba, whose name is Aramaic for "Son of the Star" was a false Messiah. Many Hebrew Primacists feel that the Bar Kokba letters prove somehow that Jesus spoke only Hebrew, despite the fact that they were written 100 years after the time of Christ and that as many of the Bar Kokhba letters are Aramaic as are Hebrew. Thus we see that Hebrew speakers, such as those among the Dead Sea Scroll community and Bar Kokhba and his circles, also spoke Aramaic. The reason they used Aramaic in addition to Hebrew is because Aramaic was the common language. Bar Kokba's "Sukkot" or "Feast of Tabernacles" letter, in which he requests the items needed to observe the Jewish Feast of Tabernacles, is in Aramaic.

In *"Bar Kokhba: The rediscovery of the legendary hero of the last Jewish Revolt Against Imperial Rome"* Yigael Yadin notes, "It is interesting that the earlier documents are in Aramaic while the later ones are in Hebrew. Possibly the change was made by a special decree of Bar-Kokhba who wanted to restore Hebrew as the official language of the state" (page 181). Yadin reveals what this opposition to Aramaic coming from certain Israelis and from certain so-called Messianic Jews is really all about. Let us look at what Yadin says on page 124 of his book on Bar Kokhba:

> The first thing that struck us was that for no apparent reason some of the letters were written in Aramaic and some in Hebrew. Jews at that period were versed in both languages, yet since most of the letters were in Aramaic, possibly Hebrew had just lately been revived by a Bar-Kokhba decree. I remembered that when I showed the letters to Mr. Ben-Gurion, then the Prime Minister, only the Aramaic documents had yet been opened. "Why did they write in Aramaic and not Hebrew?" was his immediate angry reaction, as if the scribes had been members of his staff.

So, we see that the opposition to Aramaic is not based on critical examination of the evidence but rather is based on nationalistic pride! Ben-Gurion was angry to be exposed to archeological evidence that Jews in the late first and early second century (and obviously earlier) spoke Aramaic. It didn't fit in with his fantasies about the past. We should be careful about letting ethnic pride distort the facts of history. I have heard of Greeks becoming angry when told that Alexander the Great was not Greek (Macedonians apparently were Celtic although they were Hellenizers) or that Alexander engaged in homosexual behavior. Some scholars believe that Queen Nefertiti was not a native Egyptian. This makes certain Egyptians angry. (Some scholars have found indications that Nefertiti was not a native Egyptian. Other Egyptologists have found indications that she was. The preponderance of evidence should be used to draw conclusions and not nationalistic pride.) We should look to the evidence and not allow the foolish histrionics of Ben-Gurion and those like these people who idealize instead of investigate the past to impede us on our quest for the facts.

Ossuaries (what are basically tombstones)

Ossuaries are often inscribed in Aramaic. Some are inscribed in Greek and some are in Hebrew. Important Aramaic ossuaries include the ossuary of

Caiphas and the controversial "James the Brother of Jesus" ossuary. The Talpiot Ossuaries are also Aramaic and controversial. (Yeshua was a common name and other Jesus son of Joseph ossuaries have been discovered.) Much of the evidence including the evidence from the Aramaic can be viewed in the excellent book by Craig A. Evans entitled *Jesus and the Ossuaries: What Jewish Burial Practices Reveal about the Beginning of Christianity*. (At the time of Jesus, the bodies of the dead were laid to rest inside of caves that were closed with a large flat round stone that was rolled over to over the opening of the cave. After a period of time, when the body had decayed, a relative would take the bones and place then in a small stone box that was kept in the cave. These boxes that encased the bones were called ossuaries and they often bear inscriptions upon them. Very often these inscriptions found on ossuaries are in Aramaic.)

Business records and legal archives, marriage contracts, divorce decrees and promissory notes.

Business was conducted in Aramaic. Sebastian Brock describes important discovery that gives us important insight into everyday life. Aramaic "was also the language of the delivery man at a village called Beit Qarnayim (otherwise unknown, but evidently near Jerusalem), as we learn from four ostraca belonging to the first half of the first century AD. On these pieces of broken pottery (which served as the equivalent of modern notebooks) he writes down in ink his deliveries of fig cakes, bread and barley, specifying year, day of the week, day of the month, and sometimes even whether it was morning of evening... Another vivid glimpse into everyday life is provided by a note scribbled on an ostracon from Masada, perhaps dating from the time of the First Jewish Revolt (AD 66-73). Someone has left a bill unpaid for far too long and in desperation his creditor, evidently the baker, sends him a note: "I beg you have pity on me and pay me the 5 silver denarii you owe me for the loaves of bread. Have pity, for I haven't got anything." It seems very strange to argue that Aramaic wasn't spoken by Jesus when business records from his lifetime are found that are written in Aramaic. The legal records of a woman named Babatha were found among the Bar Kokhba Scrolls. Many of her documents are in Aramaic. Archeologists have found Aramaic scrolls and inscriptions from the first century that show that Aramaic was the common language of the Jewish people at the time of Christ.

Evidence from ancient authorities

The "Jesus Spoke Only Hebrew" sect appeals to myth to prove their premise that Jesus only spoke Hebrew. They refer to the *Letter of Aristeas* which says "the Jews are assumed to speak Aramaic but it is a different kind." This probably refers to the fact that the Jews spoke a distinctive form of Aramaic (the Jewish dialect of Aramaic) or that their Scriptures are in Hebrew. Regardless, "The Letter of Aristeas" is clearly mythological and is not a historical source. (The *Letter of Aristeas* tells the story of how the Greek translation of the Pentateuch was made in a very fantastical manner. It argues that the Septuagint was divinely inspired in a manner equal to that of the original Hebrew text.) We should look at more reputable historical sources such as the writings of Flavius Josephus.

Josephus lived from 37 to circa 100 AD. He was a contemporary of St. Paul. He wrote about John the Baptist, Jesus, James the brother of Jesus and the fall of Jerusalem. Josephus was a priest and related to the Hasmoneans, a royal family.

In his preface to *The War of the Jews* he mentions that he originally wrote this book in Aramaic because he felt he was deficient in Greek and he also wrote it in Aramaic for the "barbarians" in Mesopotamia! (Josephus wanted non-Jewish Aramaic-speakers who lived in Babylonia and Assyria to be able to read his books. He specifically states this was part of the reason he originally composed his works in Aramaic before translating and re-writing them in Greek.)

In Antiquities III 10.6 he mentions that the Hebrew used Aramaic:

When a week of weeks has passed over after this sacrifice, (which weeks contain forty and nine days,) on the fiftieth day, which is Pentecost, but is called by the Hebrews *Asartha*, which signifies *Pentecost*, they bring to God a loaf, made of wheat flour, of two tenth deals, with leaven; and for sacrifices they bring two lambs.

In *War of the Jews* Book IV Chapter 1 Section 5 Josephus mentions a Roman soldier that was an Aramaic speaker from Syria, but not a Jew, sneaking into Jewish household and listening to the Jewish rebels discussing their war-plans. They were, of course, speaking in Aramaic. Josephus specifically notes that this soldier was sent on this mission, because, as he was an Aramaic speaker, he spoke the same language that the Jews did. (Josephus was often used by the Romans to speak to the masses of the Jewish people on their behalf and it is obvious that when he describes himself as doing so, he was speaking to them in Aramaic.)

According to the Talmud, there were silver trumpets in the temple into which people deposited their offerings. The offering trumpets were labeled in Aramaic, which is not surprising since they are dealing with money! When it comes to getting their money the Temple establishment made sure that these ornate offering buckets were inscribed in the plain language, Aramaic. We also have three epistles written by Rabban Gamaliel, the Rabbi who instructed Paul. They were meant for the Jewish community in the Holy Land and are written in Aramaic. Another important ancient document from the times of the apostles called "the roll of the fasts" is also written in Aramaic. The reason these documents were written in Aramaic is because they were intended to instruct the common people of the land of Israel how to properly observe the Jewish religion. Aramaic was used because it was important that these documents were understood by the greatest number of people.

Evidence from the early Church Fathers

The Hebrew Primacists sect's main argument is that the Greek word "Hebraidi" means the language that we in English know as Hebrew and can only mean Hebrew. Look at John 19:17

And He, bearing His cross, went out to a place called the Place of a Skull, which is called in Hebrew, Golgotha.

To which the Hebrew Primacist says "See it says "Hebrew" that settles it-Jesus spoke Hebrew and not Aramaic. A LAW OF LINGUISTICS: CONTEXT DETERMINES THE MEANING OF A WORD, I.E. HOW A WORD IS USED DETERMINES IT'S MEANING. (Context determines what a word is used not rhymes, acronyms or even etymologies.) In this case Golgotha is an Aramaic word. Also, the language we know as "Hebrew" is never called "Hebrew" in the Old Testament, it is called "Judean" and "Canaanite." (2 Kings 18:26, Isaiah 19:18). The Church Fathers state that Jesus and the Apostles spoke "Hebrew." Did they mean Aramaic or the language we know today as Hebrew? Papias was an early church father that interviewed people who had known the apostles. He wrote his book sometime around 110-140 AD. It has only survived in fragments. Some of his stories seem interesting or plausible, such as stories about Barsabas and that of the daughters of Phillip the Evangelist. On the other hand he describes Judas Iscariot as being so fat he was wider than a chariot and that he couldn't walk through a door and mentions Jesus saying that in the Millennium grapes will call out to people saying "Take me, take me!" These particular stories seem absurd and very different from stories we find in the Gospels in the New Testament. (Certain church fathers did not view Papias as a reliable source.) Papias gives a legend that Matthew originally wrote his Gospel in "Hebrew." Hebrew Primacists seize on this as proof that Jesus spoke Hebrew exclusively. Jerome (lived 347-420) knew of and described the "Hebrew" Matthew.

Matthew, also called Levi, apostle and aforetimes publican, composed a gospel of

Christ at first published in Judea in Hebrew for the sake of those of the circumcision who believed, but this was afterwards translated into Greek though by what author is uncertain. The Hebrew itself has been preserved until the present day in the library at Caesarea which Pamphilus so diligently gathered. I have also had the opportunity of having the volume described to me by the Nazarenes of Beroea, a city of Syria, who use it. In this it is to be noted that wherever the Evangelist, whether on his own account or in the person of our Lord the Saviour quotes the testimony of the Old Testament he does not follow the authority of the translators of the Septuagint but the Hebrew...

Jerome, *Lives of Illustrious Men*

In the Gospel according to the Hebrews, which is written in the Chaldee and Syrian [meaning "Aramaic" in contemporary English] language, but in Hebrew characters, and is used by the Nazarenes to this day (I mean the Gospel according to the Apostles, or, as is generally maintained, the Gospel according to Matthew, a copy of which is in the library at Caesarea), we find ... .

Jerome, *Against the Pelagians*

Chaldean and Syrian are other ways of saying Aramaic. (Aram is an old way of saying Syria. In Daniel 2:4 the Chaldeans, Babylonian magicians and astrologers, are quoted speaking in Aramaic. For this reason Aramaic has been called Chaldee, or "Chaldean," in the past, as we see in Strong's Exhaustive Concordance to the Holy Bible. In the King James Bible Aramaic is called "Syriack." Aramaic, Syrian and Syriac are really equivalent terms. Nevertheless, in modern usage Syriac refers to the official dialect of Aramaic used by Aramaic Christians for liturgical purposes. Syriac Aramaic is a very important form of Aramaic and we have many ancient documents in this dialect of Aramaic, including the Bible and numerous biblical commentaries. Modern Aramaic Christians use Syriac during church services but speak a Modern form of Aramaic that didn't directly emerge from Syriac.) Also, in Jerome's "Commentary to the Book of Daniel" he uses the words Aramaic and Hebrew interchangeably almost immediately after differentiating between the two languages!

Jerome, in his commentary on the Book of Daniel, differentiates between Hebrew and Aramaic, but then while in the Aramaic section of the Book of Daniel, consistently calls Aramaic "Hebrew." This proves that the early church fathers did call the language we know as Aramaic "Hebrew" at times and used "Hebrew" and other words for Aramaic interchangeably. This is illustrated by the following quotations from

Jerome's commentary on the Book of Daniel the Prophet:

> Verse 4. *"The Chaldeans replied to the king in Syriac."* Up to this point what we have read has been recounted in Hebrew. From this point on until the vision of the third year of King Balthasar [Belshazzar] which Daniel saw in Susa, the account is written in Hebrew characters, to be sure, but in the Chaldee language, which he here calls Syriac.

> Verse 27. *"As for the secret for which the king is asking, neither the wise men nor the magi nor the soothsayers nor the diviners are able to declare it to the king."* In place of diviners *(haruspices),* as we have rendered it, the Hebrew [sic!-Here Jerome calls the Aramaic language "Hebrew"] text has *Gazareni* [actually the Aramaic word is *gaz^{e}rin*.] which only Symmachus has rendered...

> ...follows as far as the end of the Song of the Three Youths is not contained in the Hebrew [i.e. the Aramaic. Jerome uses the word "Hebrew" for Aramaic yet again!].

> "...I, *Daniel, was much troubled with my thoughts, and my countenance was altered*

49

within me; but I preserved the word in my heart. " Up to this point the Book of Daniel was written in the Chaldee and Syriac language. All the rest that follows up to the very end of the volume we read in Hebrew.

In his book *Demonstration of the Gospel* Eusebius of Caesarea (c. 275-339) describes the Twelve Apostles as "quite common men, and barbarians [non-Greeks] to boot, with no knowledge of any tongue but Syrian." (Syrian means Aramaic.) After Jesus gives the Disciples the Great Commission and to preach his message to all the world, Eusebius has them ask, "But how...can we do it? How, pray, can we preach to the Romans? We are men bred up to use the Syrian tongue only, what language can we speak to the Greeks?" (As is noted above, the "Syrian tongue" is Aramaic, as Aram means "Syrian." See Eusbius Pamphylis Demonstration of the Gospel, in the English translation, *DE* Book III, chapters 5 and 7, cited *Dem. Ev. III. 4.44; 7.10.*) This helps us to understand that Eusebius means that Matthew wrote his Gospel originally in Aramaic when he states, "For Matthew, who had at first preached to the Hebrews, when he was about to go to other peoples, committed his Gospel to writing in his native tongue..." (Eusebius, Ecclesiastical History, Book III). Eusebius makes it very clear that the apostles spoke Aramaic only so obviously he refers to Matthew's "native tongue" he means Aramaic and not the language we now know as Hebrew. Eusebius-who is the source of our quote of Papias- was convinced that Jesus and the Apostles spoke only Aramaic! He had information available to him that we no longer possess today! This shows first, that the Greek word *"Hebraidi"* can indeed mean "Aramaic" and secondly, that the most ancient sources state unequivocally that the apostles spoke only Aramaic.

Evidence from the Targums

The entire Old Testament, with the exception of Ezra and Daniel (which are partially Aramaic already) was translated into Aramaic as the Targums. The Targums were not literal word-for-word translations but were free interpretive paraphrases. The Aramaic Targums are important because they originated from the time of Christ, and their interpretations reflect understandings of the text current with his era. Bible translators often refer to the Targums to clarify where it seems obscure in the original texts. Father Martin McNamara and Bruce Chilton have written extensively on using the Aramaic Targums to deepen our understanding of the New Testament. Martin McNamara's book is *Targum and Testament: Aramaic Paraphrases of the Hebrew Bible: A Light on the New Testament.*

In *Complete Equivalence in Bible Translation* by Dr. James D. Price he states, "The Targums are still included in the official Rabbinic Bible." The

Targums along with The Tanakh and the Talmud are considered authoritative by Modern Judaism. (The "Tanakh" is an acronym that refers to the Old Testament.) Two theologians have written extensively on the Aramaic Targums and their relevancy for New Testament studies. They are Bruce Chilton and Martin McNamara. Bruce Chilton is the author of *A Galilean Rabbi and His Bible* and *Rabbi Jesus: An Intimate Biography*. Reverend Chilton believes that most Jews in Judea and Galilee during the time of Jesus were illiterate and depended upon the oral Aramaic form of the Old Testament for their understanding of Scripture. Jesus does seem to speak of an oral culture in his sermon on the mount where he said; "You have heard it said...but I say unto you..." (Matthew 5:33). (Jesus is saying to the people here that their understanding of the Bible came from an oral tradition. The reason he said "you have heard it said" instead of "you have read it written" is because when he was addressing the multitudes, the majority of the people he was speaking to were illiterate.) In Bible times few people could read. For that few who did, very few of those could own an entire Bible. It was too expensive and without our small print and thin paper a Bible is huge, especially is it is written upon scrolls. It would take at least ten large scrolls to have a complete Bible. Since few people could read or possess a Bible this gave the scribes great power. (Jesus often spoke of the "scribes." For an example see Matthew 23:2. If everyone was a scribe at the time of Jesus there wouldn't have been a distinctive group of people called the "scribes" since everyone would have been a scribe.) The day of easy access to a Bible and widespread literacy was unimaginable to the ancients. I believe Jesus could read and write and knew the Scriptures in Hebrew but most people in the holy land contemporary with him could not. Bart Ehrman in his book *Truth and Fiction* describes how illiteracy was widespread during the time of Jesus,

> Jewish lower classes there, for the most part-farm workers, probably (notice all his parables about seeds, plants, trees, and harvests), fishermen, and the like. Did these people write accounts of his life? The problem is that ancient historians have come to realize that the vast bulk of the population of Jesus' day was illiterate, able neither to read nor to write. It is difficult to establish literacy levels in antiquity, but the most reliable study, by Columbia University professor William Harris, indicates that at the very best of times in the ancient world (for example, in Athens during the fifth century BC, the time of Socrates and Plato), only 10-15 percent of the population was even functionally literate (able to read and perhaps sign simple documents such as contracts). High literacy rates, such as we

> now experience in the modern West, were
> unheard of in antiquity, when it never would
> have occurred to government (or private)
> agencies to devote the massive resources
> required to ensuring that everyone could
> read and write (widespread literacy came
> about only with the industrial revolution).
> This means that at the best of times 85-90
> percent of a population was illiterate. Those
> who were able to read and possibly write
> (the latter requires more extensive training)
> were the upper classes with the resources
> and leisure required to educate their
> children. Literacy rates were much lower in
> an area such as rural Galilee, where most
> people were subsistence farmers, fishermen,
> or artisans, who had no need to learn their
> letters (106-107)

It may be that even Jewish children knew all the stories of the Bible. They didn't know the Bible from reading it, because few of them could read. They knew the Bible through its oral form and that for them was the Aramaic Targum Bible. We should be cautious about using rabbinical sources such as the Talmud. The Talmud was written over two hundred years after the time of Jesus. The Rabbis that composed it lived as distant from the time of Jesus as we do from the time of George Washington. Legends had time to develop. An example would be the myth that George

Washington chopped down the cherry tree and told his father, "I shall not tell a lie. I did it." The Talmud also contains legends and myth. Blindly accepting all rabbinical legends about the first century could cloud our understanding of the Jesus of history. In the January/February 2008 edition of Biblical Archeological Review, Richard Elliot Friedman wrote that the ancient rabbis "did not know more than we do about the Biblical world or about history or about the Bible's authors. They knew less." Certain famous Rabbis of long ago never saw the Holy Land and didn't understand its geography. The old Rabbis didn't have important archeological discoveries we now have. Sciences, such as linguistics, had yet to develop. In certain way, the rabbis understood Hebrew less than we do today because we now have the cuneiform tablets in the Ugarit language. These relics actually help us to understand biblical Hebrew better. Ugarit is very similar to Hebrew and has helped clarify the meaning of certain obscure words and phrases in the Old Testament. (Ancient translations of the Bible, such as the Septuagint, the Targums, the Syriac Peshitta, the Samaritan Pentateuch and the Latin Vulgate, often preserve the original reading of the Bible in places where the Rabbis have preserved a scribal error. These ancient texts, must be, and are, consulted by translators of the Bible.) There may be useful information in rabbinical sources but they must be used with extreme caution. The rabbis have a legend that all Jewish boys at the time of Jesus could read and write. This is very unlikely. Saint Jerome, who lived from 342-420, stated, "There doesn't exist any Jewish child who doesn't know by heart the history from Adam to Zerubbabel" What this means is that all Jewish children knew stories of the entire Bible by heart. Jerome did not say that all Jewish children were all scribes who could all read and write. He merely stated that they all knew the stories of the Bible. Most of these boys and girls learned these Bible stories through oral tradition and usually this was through the reciting of the Targum during synagogue services. A better source, one that is contemporary with the time of the Apostles, is Josephus. Describing the Jewish people, Josephus states, "Above all we pride ourselves on the education of our children, and regard as the most essential task in life the observance of our laws and of the pious practices based thereupon, which we have inherited" (*Against Apion* 1:60). Here again we see that Josephus isn't claiming that every Jewish male could read. He is stating that they teach all their children how to observe Jewish customs. Ancient scrolls are dated by what is called "paleography," which is the study of the changes in scripts throughout history. James Vanderkam and Peter Flint explain how ancient documents, such as the Dead Sea Scrolls, are dated in *The Meaning of the Dead Sea Scrolls: Their Significance for Understanding the Bible, Judaism, Jesus and Christianity*. They say, "Few people in antiquity could write, and the few who did most of

56

the writing were trained in the standard accepted ways of forming letters. Not all writers were professional scribes, but many were, so that there was little of the massive variety in writing styles that we see today when so many more people are literate. Moreover, it probably means that changes in scripts took some time to develop; the scribal art favored conservatism over innovation." The reality that very few people could read and write helps scientists accurately date ancient documents. Jewish myths about universal literacy do not accurately reflect the historical reality and the oral culture in which Christianity emerged. We need to employ a healthy skepticism when dealing with certain rabbinical sources. It is best to rely on more ancient evidence such as archeological discoveries and texts such as Josephus and Philo that date to the time of Christ and the Apostles. (However, we shouldn't view even Josephus and Philo as inerrant and infallible. Josephus as a supporter of Rome had his own biases and his own agenda. Philo was a Hellenistic Jew, which was common for Jews in the Roman Empire who lived outside of the Holy Land. Josephus and Philo do reflect the viewpoints, culture and traditions of Jewish people of the New Testament period in a way that rabbinical writings written centuries later do not.)

Jesus actually quoted from the Aramaic Targum of Psalm 22 when he was in agonizing pain and approaching death upon the cross.(There are other verses of Scripture where Jesus and Paul quote from the Aramaic Targum version of the Old Testament.) He was repeating the oral form of scripture he had learned as a child in synagogue. It is most likely that at such a time as that he would be speaking his first language. Those that argue that Jews at the time of Jesus spoke only Hebrew state that they were fluent in Hebrew yet would discuss and interpret the Scriptures in Aramaic, which according to the "Hebrew Primacists," was a language few could understand. I find it hard to believe that people would discuss their literature in a language they didn't speak. Where is the logic in that? This is like saying, we are all native English speakers but we are going to translate and discuss Milton in French! And we are going to do this merely to discuss Milton. That is absurd! The more logical explanation is that the Jews needed translations of their Scriptures in Aramaic because few still spoke Hebrew fluently. The Targums were believed to have been an oral tradition that was passed down and not written until centuries after the time of Jesus. Now we have Targumim found among the Dead Sea Scrolls. And Paul quotes from the Targums too. What Hebrew primacists are doing is attempting to dismiss the authority of the Sacred Scriptures. If everyone is speaking Hebrew as their mother tongue-then who is speaking Aramaic? Why would they speak Aramaic and when? For a monastery library where Hebrew is seen as the holy language and the language of education-there are a lot of documents in a language Hebrew Primacists say wasn't spoken-1/5 of the scrolls are in Aramaic! (Perhaps an equivalent example could be a monastery library in Europe in the Middle Ages. Almost all books then were written in Latin, a language few could understand. The "vulgar," or common, languages were rarely written until the time of Dante. One fifth of the books in Aramaic in a library where Hebrew was viewed as the sacred language is a huge number and shows that the people spoke Aramaic as their common language.) The Apostles had Aramaic names and Jesus gave out Aramaic nicknames-why, if he wasn't an Aramaic speaker? If Jesus spoke Hebrew as his first language then when and why would he use Aramaic at all? I frankly cannot understand that irrational hostility against Aramaic coming from Hebrew Primacists. It seems to me that Hebrew was spoken in some circles but for most of the common people it was an acquired language. Although the Targum represented a traditional oral understanding of the Bible at the time of Jesus, and most copies of the Targum were written centuries after the time of Jesus, we do have written Targums that date to the time of Jesus. Mainstream Christian Jews do not carry this irrational hostility towards the Aramaic language. The Messianic organization "Jews for Jesus" recognizes the importance of the Targumim and have often referenced them in their publications.

A note about scholarly consensus

The vast majority of Bible scholars believe Jesus spoke Aramaic because this fact is borne out by the evidence-which is cumulative. We should take mainstream and not extremist positions. The "Jesus spoke only Hebrew" position is an extremist position and cannot withstand scrutiny. Certain people believe that Jesus spoke Hebrew because Hebrew is viewed by them as the language of God. Jesus is God Incarnate and he spoke Aramaic so, Aramaic could also be viewed as the language of God! (Daniel mentions the finger of God writing on the wall of the palace in Babylonia in the Aramaic language. Also, in the Talmud there is a story of God speaking out in Aramaic from the Holy of Holies. This was during the High Priesthood of John Hyrcanus. See. *J. Sot. 24b*.) As Jesus proclaimed his Gospel in Aramaic, Aramaic is also the language of the Kingdom of God. According to Deuteronomy 26:5, Abraham and the Patriarchs were Aramaic speaking. In the Talmud (*b. Sanhedrin 38b*) the Rabbis teach that God spoke Aramaic to Adam and Eve in the Garden of Eden-and that Aramaic was the language of Adam! If Jesus actually spoke Aramaic, then to attack, disparage and insult his language is to attack and insult Jesus Christ himself.

In *Language, Power and Identity in Ancient Palestine*, Seth Swartz states,

From 300 B.C.E. to 70 C.E., Hebrew was no longer commonly spoken, having been replaced by Aramaic. Hebrew, however, remained important because it was still the language of the Jerusalem temple and of the Pentateuch. In part because of consistent imperial patronage, these institutions gradually became the central symbols of Jewish corporate identity in the three or four centuries after their respective foundation (c. 500 B.C.E.) and compilation (c.400 B.C.E.). By the third century B.C.E., Hebrew began to be used on coins and the like in a way which may have been intended to evoke these symbols, and thus Jewish identity. But the temple and the Torah also became real repositories of power, so that there developed around both of them closely related classes of curators. These men used Hebrew to distinguish themselves from the rest of the population, and since curatorship of the Torah was in theory open to all males, mastery of Hebrew was also a path to prestige, and study of it was widespread in certain circles. In this second stage then, Hebrew, no longer commonly spoken, became a commodity, consciously manipulated by the leaders of the Jews to evoke the Jews' distinctness from their

neighbours, and the leaders' own
distinctness from their social inferiors.

According to Seth Swartz, Aramaic was the
language of the common Jew but Hebrew was used
by the elite. Mr. Swartz also states, "In sum, the
evidence from Palestine in the sixth to the third
centuries B.C.E. is consistent with the view that the
Jews, like almost all other national and tribal groups
in the Levant and Mesopotamia, generally came to
adopt Aramaic as their normal means of
communication. The contrary view is based on a
simplistic reading of the evidence, characterized by
insensitivity to its content and context, and
correspondingly to the social and political functions
of languages in pre-modern societies." When
someone makes sensational or extreme claims, such
as the claim that Jesus did not speak Aramaic, our
first demand is to examine the evidence. What kind
of argument is this person making? Can the
argument withstand scrutiny? We should also ask
questions. Who is making the claim? What
institution is he affiliated with? What kind of
accreditation does the institution have? Has this
theory been peer reviewed? What do other
authorities and experts say? Are there arguments or
is there evidence that contradicts this theory? What
are the motivations or biases of this individual
making these claims? The reason most Bible
scholars believe Jesus spoke Aramaic is because
that is what the Bible says and there is also other

extra-biblical information that indicates that this is true. We should be wary of extremism.

I have heard Zephaniah 3:9 used to say that we all must learn to speak Hebrew in order to be acceptable to God. This scripture reads, "For I will restore to the people a pure language" (literally the Hebrew says a "pure lip" this means pure speech or conversation and is not necessarily referring to a specific language) "that they all may call upon the name of the Lord, to serve him with one accord." Jesus spoke about the same thing when he said "From the abundance of the heart the mouth speaks" (Matthew 12:34). It is unreasonable to require all believers to learn Hebrew, or Aramaic for that matter. (Although, it would be good to take steps to preserve Aramaic as a spoken language.) This passage in Zephaniah actually refers to God giving his people a new heart-a truth Jesus and other prophets of the Old Testament refer to. (At any rate, Hebrew isn't a "pure language." Modern Hebrew especially has strong Russian, English and Arabic influences. Hebrew, like all languages, evolved. This evolution of the language can be seen in the text of the Old Testament. Even in the Hebrew of the Old Testament, we see the influence of other languages on Hebrew. This includes not only Aramaic, but also Greek and Persian words are found in the Hebrew of the Old Testament. Words we think of as "Hebrew" such as Sanhedrin and Synagogue are Greek words that found their way into Hebrew. Ancient Israel's pagan neighbors, the Edomites, Moabites, and Phoenicians all spoke Hebrew. The idea that speaking a particular language makes a person holier or more pleasing to God is illogical.) To understand God you need to come with him with childlike faith and simplicity. Learning a language will not get you into heaven and may not even please God. In ancient times there were and today there are many Hebrew speakers who are terrible sinners and don't know God. (According to this faction of Messianics it is only Hebrew speakers that are capable of understanding and pleasing God. Certain of these Hebrew Primacists people also believe that only those with Jewish blood will go to Heaven.) Hannibal and the Carthaginians spoke a form of Hebrew as did many of the ancient Israelites who worshiped Baal and the Ashtorah. Nicodemus knew Hebrew, Aramaic and the Scriptures and Jewish tradition. Jesus wasn't impressed with all of this. Jesus was concerned about his soul-because Nicodemas was lost. Jesus told him "For a man to enter into the Kingdom of God he must be born again." (The Gospel of John Chapter Three. It seems to me on the basis of the later actions of Nicodemas, that he did receive Jesus and was born-again.) This faction of Messiancis are requiring people to become full proselytes to Judaism and come to speak Hebrew in order to be acceptable to God. We must preach the simplicity of the Gospel. These "Hebrew-Only" people are harming the body of Christ and confusing the

Gospel message. (It is hard to consider Hebrew a "pure" language. It evolved out of previous Semitic language and continued to evolve throughout the biblical period. Even today Modern Hebrew is significantly different from Biblical Hebrew and is continuing to evolve.) It is good to learn Biblical languages but it isn't required in order to go to heaven. As Paul the Apostle said, "Knowledge puffs up but love edifies."

Jesus is the Son of David, but the title called Himself most often was the Son of Man. Jesus is the Son of all Mankind and the savior of humanity. (Matthew's Gospel mentions gentiles in Jesus' family tree.) Jesus says when he comes in power and glory to judge the world he doesn't judge the people on if they kept Kosher, or if they observed the Sabbath, or if they spoke Hebrew or were "Torah observant"-the concern is did they show love and compassion to "the least of these my brethren" (Matthew 25). The Lord requires mercy-not sacrifice. Paul in 1 Corinthians 13 says, you can have all knowledge-even perfect knowledge of Hebrew-but if you don't have love-it is NOTHING! The Hebrew and Aramaic roots of our faith are important –but nothing should be allowed to complicate the simple message of Salvation preach by Jesus and the Apostles. The reason that the majority of Bible scholars believe that Jesus spoke in Aramaic is because this is what is indicated by the evidence and the Bible clearly and repeatedly states this to be true. When scholars state that Jesus spoke Aramaic they are simply stating fact and are not trying to displace or disparage Hebrew. As Hebrew is the original language of over 95% of the Old Testament it's importance is firmly established. Those who deny that Christ spoke the language that the Bible even quotes him speaking believe that the Holy Bible is erroneous and not a faithful record of the life and ministry of Jesus the Messiah.

Abba, Father

Jesus called upon God as "Abba, Father," in his Aramaic language. Understanding this concept is crucial to understanding the message of Jesus, his concept of God. When we do this we are looking at the most primitive source we have on Jesus the Messiah and his conception of who God is. This most primitive source is the actual Aramaic words he originally spoke as he originally spoke them. Who was God to Jesus? Did Jesus worship God as the "Sacred Feminine" as Dan Brown, the author of *The Da Vinci Code* claims? The answer to this question is found in the Aramaic word Jesus used to call upon God when he prayed. The first thing we need to do is to define this Aramaic word, Abba. This Aramaic word found its way into Hebrew and is now the Hebrew word for 'Daddy'. The Hebrew word for Father is Avi. In Modern Aramaic the pronunciation of Abba has changed and now it is 'baba'. The Aramaic word "Abba" is found three times in the Greek New Testament. Jesus cries out to "Abba, Father" in the Garden of Gethsemane. Paul uses the Aramaic word 'Abba' twice in his epistles. This is significant because Paul rarely uses Aramaic in his epistles. The only other two Aramaic words he uses is "Maranatha" for "Come, O Lord" and he refers to Simon by the Aramaic form of his name "Cephas" more often than the Greek form "Peter". The word "abba" is significant because it comes from the lips of Jesus Christ himself. St. Paul thought it was significant enough to expand on this word and include it in two of his epistles. The idea of the Fatherhood of God is a distinctive Christian teaching. Islam totally rejects the idea of the Fatherhood of God. Mohammad in his Koran totally rejects the idea that God is our Father or that anyone is in any way a child of God. In Islam "Allah has 99 Names" but not one of these names is "Father."

Jews did not and do not address God as 'abba'. There is however one old story from the first century of a Rabbi who did refer to God as Abba.

> Hannan He-Nehba was the son of the daughter of Onias the Circle-drawer. When the world needed rain, our teachers used to send school-children to him, who seized the hem of his coat and said to him "Abba, Abba, Hab Lan Mitra" (Aramaic for 'Daddy, Daddy, give us rain!") He said to Him (God) 'Master of the world, grant it for the sake of these who are not yet able to distinguish between an Abba who has the power to give rain and an abba who does not."

(This story calls to mind certain teachings of Jesus. Jesus says that the Father knows what children need in Matthew 6:32. He tells us that the Father sends rain on the just and the unjust in Matthew 5:25. We are also told that the father gives good gifts to his children who ask of him in Matthew 7:11.)

In ancient records there is an isolated instance of an adult referring to his father as "Abba". This does not mean that Abba does not mean 'Daddy'. My mother called her father 'daddy' until his death. (In old Aramaic 'Abba' is 'daddy' and 'abhi' is 'father'.) Some rabbis used 'abba' as a title. Jesus, perhaps partly for this reason, said, "Call no man 'father' on earth" (Matthew 23:9). An equivalent to Abba is perhaps "papa" as well as "daddy". In certain languages the Roman Catholic pope is addresses as papa, which is what the word 'pope' is derived from. In the Targums, the Aramaic version of the Old Testament, it is seen that the Jews deliberately avoided using the word Abba to refer to God.

In The Books and the Parchments *F.F. Bruce makes an interesting note about ABBA; Aramaic for "Daddy"*

> We read in Mark 14:36 how Jesus prayed in the Garden of Gethsemane, 'Abba, Father, all things are possible unto thee'. While Abba is an Aramaic word, it made its way into Hebrew use as well; to this day a Hebrew-speaking boy will address his father as Abba. But in addressing God, Jews did not and do not employ this form, the affectionate term for intimate use within the family, but the more formal Abi, 'my Father', or Abinu, 'Our Father'. Jesus,

however, or set purpose used the intimate and affectionate from Abba when addressing God, and His example was followed by the early Christians, who used the same Aramaic word. So Paul, in Rom. 8:15 and Gal. 4:6, reckons it a sign that God has sent the Spirit of His Son, 'the spirit of son-ship, into the hearts of believers in Christ when they pray 'Abba, Father'. Many grandiloquent phrases are often employed in addressing God in prayer and worship but none of them is so Christian as the simple 'Abba, Father', used by our Lord.

In the Greek New Testament the Greek word pater, which means "father," is used to explain the Aramaic word Abba. If pater captured the full meaning of the Aramaic word abba, what is the point for using the Aramaic word in the first place? If abba merely means pater, or "father," why is it used so many times? If abba merely meant 'father' the Aramaic term wouldn't have been used at all. William Barclay believed that Abba is un-translatable. According to Barclay,

> There is extraordinary intimacy which Jesus put into the term. Jesus called God, *Abba*, Father" (Mark 14:36). As Jeremias points out there is not even the remotest parallel to this in all Jewish literature. *Abba*, like the modern Arabic *jaba*, is the word used by a

young child to his father. It is the ordinary, everyday family word which a little child used in speaking to his father. It is completely untranslatable. Any attempt to put it into English ends in bathos or grotesqueness. It is a word which no one had ever ventured to use in addressing God before.

For Jesus the fatherhood of God was something of almost inexpressible sacredness, and it was something of unsurpassable tender intimacy. In it is summed up everything that he came to say about God in this relationship with men.

When we set this conception of God as the Father, to whom a man may go with the same confidence and trust as a child goes to his earthly father, beside the Jewish conception of the remote transcendence of God and beside the Greek conceptions of the grudging God, the gods who are unaware of our existence, the god without a heart, we see it is indeed true that Jesus brought men good news about God.

So, why did Jews avoid using Abba in reference to God? Joachim Jeremias explained this in his book *The Central Message of the New Testament:*

> The reason why Jewish prayers do not address God as Abba is disclosed when one

considers the linguistic background of the word. Originally, abba was a babbling sound. The Talmud says: 'When a child experiences the taste of wheat (that is, when it is weaned) it learned to say [in Aramaic] abba and imma (that is, Dada and Mama are the first words it utters); and the church fathers Chrysostom, Theodore of Mopsuestia, and Theodoret of Cyrus, all three of them born in Antioch of well-to-do parents, but in all probability raised by [Aramaic-speaking] Syrian nurses, tell us of their own experience that little children used to call their fathers abba.

Abba means Daddy. It seems almost irreverent to address God, who is seen as distant and sanctimonious, in such an intimate and loving way. But this is what Jesus dared to do and what he dares us to do. That is to have an intimate loving relationship with almighty God.

God as Father

Christ's teaching of the Fatherhood of God was a radical new message but it did have an Old Testament precedent. God referred to the nation of Israel as his son. Moses said to Pharaoh, "Thus saith the Lord, Israel is my Son, even my first-born. And I say unto thee, "Let My son go, that he may serve me" (Exodus 4: 22) There are other important scriptures were God is the father to the nation of Israel.

> Yet, O Lord, thou art Our Father,
> We are the clay, and thou are our potter
(Isaiah 64:8)

> A son honors his father,
> And a servant his master.
> If I am a Father, where is my honor?
> If I am a master, where is my fear (Malachi
1:6)

An important passage shows that God in the Old Testament desired to have a relationship with Israel as a Father, but this desire was rejected by Israel and had to wait until the proclamation of the Good News of the Kingdom of God by Jesus Christ.

> I thought how I would set you among my
> sons,
> And give you a pleasant land,
> A heritage most beauteous of all nations.
> And I thought you would call me, My
> Father,
> And would not turn from following me.
> Surely, as a faithless wife leaves her
> husband,
> So you have been faithless to me, O house
> of Israel (Jeremiah 3: 19)

According to Ben Witherington Yahweh desired to have the Fatherly relationship with Israel but He was resisted and this relationship that God desired with his people was rejected by the nation of Israel and hence this revelation had to await the coming of the Messiah. As Ben Witherington III states in *The Shadow of the Almighty: Father, Son and Spirit in the Biblical Perspective*:

> We may also with to point to several prophetic texts as possible exceptions to the rule about [not] naming God as Father in the OT. In Jeremiah 3:19 God's people are upbraided with the words: "I thought you would call me, my Father, and would not turn from following me." The implication is that God's people have not addressed God in this way, though it was something God had hoped for. Notice too here the connection with the estrangement from God. Instead of having an intimate relationship with God characterized in familial terms, just the opposite was happening. Israel was turning away from God and ceasing to follow Gods ways. Jer. 31:9 also emphasized that it is God's own earnest desire to relate to his people as a father. He will protect those returning from exile "for I am a father to Israel, and Ephraim [Ephraim was the prominent northern Israelite tribe] is my firstborn."

The Davidic King was considered the Son of God in a special way. Of the Son of David God spoke and said, "I will be his Father, and he shall be my Son" (2 Samuel 7:14). This is Messianic is significance and is why Jesus was called Bar-Dawood, the Son of David. He had the right to call God his Father. This special prerogative of the Son of David, the Messiah, is seen also in Psalm 2. In the Targum of Psalm 89:27, God promises the future anointed Davidic King that he will call on God saying, "You are abba to me, my God!" In ancient Judaism only the king that was of the dynasty of King David, could dare call upon God as Father. But as Joachim Jeremias says, with Jesus' doctrine of Abba; "We are confronted with something new and unheard of which breaks through the limits of Judaism. *Here we see who the historical Jesus was: the man who had the power to address God and Abba and who included sinners and the publicans in the kingdom by authorizing them to repeat this one word, 'Abba, Dear Father'.*

With Dan Brown's book *The Da Vinci Code* attention has been given to the so-called 'sacred feminine'. Some people feel that it is no longer appropriate to refer to God as Father much less as Daddy (Abba). My interest is to explore what Jesus taught and believed about the nature of God and not shifting fads in our contemporary society. In our scriptures God reveals himself in a masculine gender. This is divine revelation and has nothing to do with "sexism." Jesus taught the Fatherhood of God but his consideration of women is seen in his life and ministry. To protect women and the family he discouraged divorce (Matthew 5:32). He taught women the mysteries of the Kingdom of God (Luke 10: 39, John 4: 10-15) and he took women as disciples (Luke 8: 2-3). These women traveled with Jesus and supported his ministry.

IT IS IMPORTANT TO NOTE THAT GOD'S ETERNAL NATURE IS THAT OF A FATHER. God is about relationships. That is why he desires relationship with people. God's eternal triune nature is about a relationship between the Father, the Son and the Holy Spirit. At Ephesians 3:14 St. Paul states, "For this reason I bow my knees before the Father of our Lord Jesus Christ from whom all fatherhood in heaven and earth is named." This is a direct translation from the Greek. Most modern translations, including the King James Version, read "every family" rather than "all fatherhood". The original Greek has "all fatherhood". God as "Our Father" has been an established Christian doctrine but now this central tenet of the Christian faith is being called into question. In *The Promise of the Father: Jesus and God in the New Testament* Marianne Meye Thompson attempts to minimize the significance of Christ's teachings on God as our Father. Thompson is a revisionist trying to develop a new unorthodox feminist theology. Thompson argues that there was nothing new, unique or revolutionary in Christ's teaching of God as Father and that it had all been stated in Judaism before. She attempts to dismiss this teaching as irrelevant and presents this doctrine as merely echoes of primitive near eastern tribal barbaric culture. She even attacks the Lord's Prayer and states that it she finds it offensive since it "excludes" people. In her book she also attacks the research of the great Aramaic expert and Bible scholar Joachim Jeremias. Besides being factually incorrect, Thompson's views are in conflict with the teaching of the New Testament and also with Christian tradition. A rebuttal to her book is found in *The Shadow of the Almighty: Father, Son and Spirit in the Biblical Perspective* by Ben Witherington III and Laura M. Ice.

Despite the claims of Thompson, it is evident that the Father/Son relationship is important in the very identity of God. Andrew Murray makes this clear in *With Christ in the School of Prayer*. Murray describes this as the Key to the Mystery of the Holy Trinity. It explains that the reason that God desires relationships and prayer from us is that his eternal nature and person is that of such relationships. Murray states,

> Seeking answers to such questions provides the key to the very being of God in the mystery of the Holy Trinity. If God were only one Person, shut up within Himself, there could be no thought of nearness to Him or influence on Him. But in God there

are three Persons: *Father, Son* and *Holy Spirit.* It is in the Holy Spirit that the Father and Son have their living bond of unity and fellowship. When the Father gave the Son a place next to Himself as His equal and His counselor, He opened a way for prayer and its influence into the very inmost life of the Trinity itself...As the representative of all creation, Christ always has a voice in the Father's decisions. In the decrees of the eternal purpose, room is always left for the liberty of the Son and mediator and intercessor. The same holds true for the petitions of all who draw near to the Father through the Son.

Murray illustrates that the Infinite Fatherliness of God is an indispensable doctrine, fundamental in the message of salvation and crucial in prayer. Concerning the Father-hood of God in the message of repentance and salvation Murray states

Jesus came to baptize with the Holy Spirit, who could not stream forth until Jesus was glorified. When Jesus made an end of sin, He entered into the Holiest of All with His blood. There on our behalf he received the Holy Spirit and sent Him down to us as the Spirit of the Father. It was when Christ had redeemed us and we had received the position of children that the Father sent the Spirit of His Son into our hearts to cry; "Abba, Father." The worship in spirit is the worship of the Father in the Spirit of Christ, in the Spirit of son-ship. This is the reason why Jesus uses the name of Father here. We never find one of the Old Testament saints personally appropriating the name of child in relationship to God or calling God their Father. The worship of *the Father* is only possible for those to whom the Spirit of the Son has been given. The worship *in spirit* is only possible for those to whom the Son has revealed the Father, and who receive the spirit of son-ship. It is only Christ who opens the way and teaches the worship in spirit.

Jeremias also illustrates this fact saying,

Judaism had a great wealth of forms of address to God at its disposal. For example, the 'Prayer", Tephilla, (later called the Eighteen Benedictions), which was already prayed three times a day in the New Testament period, ends each benediction with a new form of address to God...It can be seen here that one form of address to God is put after another. If we were to collect all the forms of address that appear in early Jewish prayer literature, we would find ourselves with a very extensive lest. Nowhere, however, in the Old Testament do we see God being addressed as 'Father"…In post-canonical Jewish literature there are isolated examples of the use of pater as an address to God; these. However come from Diaspora Judaism, which is here following the influence of the Greek world. In Palestine, it is only in the early Christian period that we come across two prayers which use 'Father' as an address to God, both in the form abinu malkenu. But it should be noted that these are liturgical prayers in which God is addressed as the Father of the community…the Father to whom the community calls is the heavenly king of the people of God…It is quite unusual that Jesus should have addressed God as 'my Father"; it is even more so that he should have used the Aramaic form Abba.

Jeremias's point is still well established despite Thompson's efforts to discredit him. She finally admits near the end of her book, "it is particularly striking that no passage in the Old Testament gives an account in which God names himself as Father." This revelation of God's nature was only hinted at in the Old Testament. Jesus brought the full revelation of God's eternal nature of Father.

Abba's Child

In the Garden of Gethsemane Jesus prayed, "Abba, Father, all things are possible unto Thee. Take away this cup form Me; nevertheless not what I will, but what thou wilt" (Mark 14: 36). Never in Judaism before Jesus did any rabbi dare to address God as "My Father" as Jesus did. Jesus also instructed his follows to pray to Our Father as he did. The use of the word 'Abba' is very important because it is what scholars call "ipissima vox", the Original Voice, or" ipissima verbo", the authentic words. There is no doubt that his was the exact word Jesus spoke. And Jesus always prayed to God as Father. How important is this saying of Jesus? No less than 170 times in the Holy Gospels does Jesus call God 'Father'.

Abba is however a mystery, a special revelation that comes only through Jesus Christ. The Messiah said, "All things are delivered unto Me by My Father, and no man knoweth the Son, but the Father, neither knoweth any man the Father, except he Son, and he to whomsoever the Son will reveal Him" (Matthew 11: 27). Paraphrased from the Aramaic this means, "Only Father and Son truly know each other. And because only a father and a son truly know each other, therefore a son can reveal to others the innermost thoughts of his Father." So, only Jesus can pass on to others the real knowledge of God. This is further shown in John 14: 8:

Phillip said unto him, "Lord, show us the Father and it will suffice." Jesus said unto him, "Have I been so long a time with you, and yet hast thou not known me, Phillip? He that hath seen me hath seen the Father,; and how sayest thou then, 'Show us the Father'? The words that I speak unto you I speak not of myself; but the Father dwelleth in me, he doeth the works. Believe me that I am in the Father, and the Father in me...

How important is Christ's teaching about God as Abba? Joachim Jeremias goes as far as to say that Jesus "goes as far as to say that only he who can repeat this childlike Abba shall enter into the Kingdom of God. This is why Jesus says "Let the little children come unto me" (Mark 10:14) and "Unless you humble yourselves and become like little children you shall by no means enter into the Kingdom of God" (Matthew 18:3-4) and "Unless a man be born again he cannot see the Kingdom of God" (John 3:3) Repentance means a turning away from sins but for the Christian it is more than that because we believe in salvation by grace through faith and not a works based salvation. Joachim Jeremias also says, "Becoming a child again means: to learn to say Abba again. This brings us to the meaning of repentance. Repentance means learning to say Abba again, putting one's whole trust in the heavenly Father, returning to the father's house and the Father's arms…repentance of the lost son consists in his finding his way home to his father. In the last resort, repentance is simply trusting in the grace of God."

The word "Abba" was used and understood in churches that were founded by Paul, such as those in Galatia but it was also used in churches not founded by Paul, such as Rome. (The Greek word for Father is Pater.) The two passages in which Paul refers to God as Abba are very significant. The first one is Galatians 4:6

> But when the fullness of time had come, God sent forth His son, made or a woman, made under the law, to redeem those who were under the law, that we might receive adoption of Sons. And because ye are sons, God hath sent forth the Spirit of His Son into your hearts, crying, "Abba, Father." Therefore thou art no more a servant but a son, and if a son, then an heir of God through Christ.

What is important here is the agency of the Holy Spirit in adopting us into the family of God. This same theme is picked up in Romans 8: 15

> Therefore, brethren, we are debtors, not to the flesh to live according to the flesh, for if ye live according to the flesh ye shall die, but if ye through the flesh do mortify the

deeds of the body ye shall live. For as many as are led by the Spirit of God, they are the Sons of God. For we have not received the spirit of bondage again to fear, but ye have received the spirit of adoption, whereby we cry, "Abba! Father!" The Spirit itself bears witness with our sprit that we are the children of God; and if children then heirs,- heirs of God and joint heirs with Christ, if so it be that we suffer with him, that we may be also glorified together. For I reckon that the sufferings of this present time are not worthy to be compared with the glory which shall be revealed in us.

The greatest difficulty is humiliating ourselves as children. In our human nature we cannot do this, and this is why we must be born again. In both of Paul's Abba passages he notes that it is through the agency of the Holy Spirit that we are empowered to address God as "Abba". Carlo Caretto reminds us of the difficulty of becoming like a child and embracing God as Abba-Daddy.

"If you do not become like little children you shall not enter the Kingdom," and that's not easy for those who have been complicated by sin. To become like children means to increase our feeling for God's fatherhood over us, it means to think and act as little children do to the father they love.

He looks after everything, he resolves everything and so on. When does a little child ever worry about tomorrow? Never, the father takes care of it...All our plans, even on the road to holiness, are perfectly useless: the real plan is in His hand and we need to go to Him like children seeking love. I want to become little so I can run more swiftly towards the great final fire...no holding back, just trust in the immense mercy of the One who immolated His Son to save a slave."

Behold what manner of love the Father has given unto us that we may be called the Sons of God! (1 John 3:1). We were not born as the Sons of God naturally. In our original nature we are fallen. We must be born again in order to become children of God. God loves us so much. The Bible says that God is Love. God desires a relationship with us but we must be born again in order to see the Kingdom of God. We are saved by trust; that is by trusting in Jesus as our Savior. The only way to do this is to make Jesus our Lord. This is only possible by the power of the Holy Spirit. Thompson is forced to concede that,

> Paul explicitly locates the believer's address to God as "Abba, Father!" in the work of the Holy Spirit (8:15)...Paul's use of the

unusual verb "to cry" (*krazein*) has been taken to point to the emotional, enthusiastic, or spontaneous prayers of believers. At the same time, the address to God as *abba* has been read, in light of Jeremias's arguments about Jesus' use of the term, to refer to the believer's sense of intimacy in relationship with God...Paul's use of *krazein*, rather than a word for confess, speak, or pray is indeed striking. One does not confess that God is Father; one does not even pray to God as father. Rather, they 'cry' to God as Father. The term *krazein* is also found in Galatians 4:6...It seems likely, therefore, that the verb *krazein* is used because the Spirit is the ultimate source of these words , rather than because they signify the interior or emotional state of those who are speaking or a particular setting of prayer or worship.

Ben Witherington III and Laura M. Ice suggest that this occurs through the infilling of the Holy Spirit in *The Shadow of the Almighty: Father, Son, and Spirit in Biblical Perspective*. They suggest that by the Holy Spirit "Christians are enabled to cry "abba, Father!" Notice that the verb "cry" here, which suggests at the very least an earnest imploring of God, if not an ecstatic experience engendered by the Spirit...our minds also are not capable of articulating what we ought to be saying to God in prayer and so the Spirit intercedes and prays with and through the believer, with sighs too deep for words, a possible reference to glossolalia…" Glossolalia means "speaking in tongues." It is a radical supernatural experience with the Holy Spirit that enables us to cry out, like a child for her daddy, "Abba, Father!"-"Daddy, God!"

Abba's Image

God is our eternal Father. But we are not to remain children but to grow in the Lord. Paul says that, "for whom he foreknow, he also predestined to be conformed to the image of his Son, that he might be the first-born among many brethren" (Romans 8: 29). Paul says that we are to be conformed to the image of the Son of God yet he warns us, "be not conformed to this world, but be ye transformed by the renewing of your mind, that ye may prove what is good and acceptable and perfect will of God" (Romans 12: 2). We are saved and what are we saved from? Not just hell, but the hell we make of our lives with Hate, Anger, Gluttony, Greed, Indulgence, Selfishness and Sexual Sin. We are saved unto Love, Mercy, Compassion, Kindness, Joy, Happiness and unto God works. No man can serve two masters, Jesus warns us. He will either love the one and hate the other, or hold to the one and despise the other. Love the Lord, hold on to Him, make Jesus your first love. Jesus calls us to be lost in the Love of God.

The importance of the Aramaic concept of Abba is seen in a careful examination of the Greek text of the New Testament. Fatherhood is a universal concept. The idea that Jesus and the writers of the New Testament want to connect with God as Father isn't just the current cultural norms and mores of fatherhood but also the biological act of begetting. Fathers begetting is inherent in being a father no matter what culture you are born into. Frank Stagg in his *New Testament Theology* notes that, "It was Jesus' function to "bring many sons into glory" (Hebrews 2:10). He could only do this by expiating (overcoming) the sins of the people (2:17). He also identified himself with us as our brother (2:11), having fellowship (*koinonia*) with "blood and flesh, that he could break the power of sin and death for us (2:14f)." The Eternal Son of God, who is eternally begotten of the Father, took upon himself flesh so that we may be born into the family of God (Colossians 1:15). This is done by us being, as Stagg notes, *"Begotten from above"*. Stagg says, "Newness of life is described through the "birth" analogy, but probably the stronger New Testament emphasis is seen in its tracing the new life to a divine begetting. John 3:3 may best be translated; "Except one be begotten from above, he is not able to see the kingdom of God." The familiar "born again" misses the meaning at two points. The Greek *anothen* means "from above" not merely again. It is not just another beginning but a new kind of beginning that is required...Man needs more than improvement; a new destiny requires a new origin, and the new origin must be from God. But even "born from above" leaves something to be desired in translation. Probably "begotten from above" is the meaning. The Greek verb *genna*...normally...describes the father function of begetting. In effect John 3:3 may declare: "Except one be begotten of God, he is not able to see the kingdom of God." This underscores the fact that one enters the new life through an act of God. The act is not coercive, but it is essential and indispensable." Jesus identifies God as Father through the act of begetting sons and daughters and says we cannot see the kingdom of God unless we are engendered from above by the Father. Peter specifically reaffirms this is when he says, "Blessed be the God and Father of Our Lord Jesus Christ, which according to his abundant mercy hath begotten us again unto a lively hope by the resurrection of Jesus Christ from the dead" (1 Peter 1:3).

The role of fathers was crucial not only in the ministry of Jesus Christ but also of John the Baptist. Elijah is prophesied to come to prepare the way of the Messiah. According to Jesus, John the Baptist had the anointing, the spirit and the role of Elijah. Elijah will come again (Matthew 17:11) as a minister of reconciliation. This is the concluding word of the Old Testament. As it close it sets the stage for Jesus by stressing fatherhood and the coming of the Messiah.

> Look, I am going to send you Elijah the prophet before the great and awesome day of Yahweh comes. And he will turn the hearts of the fathers to their children and the hearts of the children to their fathers. Otherwise, I will come and strike the earth with a curse. (Malachi 4:5-6)

Elijah's mission is to restore fatherhood. According to the Book of Revelation, for this preaching of Elijah he will be killed and his death will be celebrated (Revelation 11:4-14). Satan hates fatherhood so much that when Jesus was calling upon God as Abba the satanic oppression against our Lord was so strong that Jesus began sweating blood (Luke 22:43-44). Satan and his forces of evil hate God. As God's eternal nature is father, Satan hates fatherhood. Satan hates mankind because Man in created in the image of his enemy, God. We are stewards of God's revelation. We do not have the right to revise, change or adapt his holy word. Those who do so, according to the scriptures, are cursed. According to the divine revelation God is our king, not our ruler nor our queen. God in his sacred voice speaks not in a neuter or feminine voice but in the male gender. God created the man, Adam, in his image. In Christ men and women are equal. Jesus revealed to mankind the perfection of the Gospel. He showed us God, not as parent, not as mother, and not only as father but as Abba, daddy, father. Since, as Ephesians declares, fatherhood is an expression of God's nature Satan hates it and wars against it. Hence we see homosexuality, single parenthood and abortion. Father's, despite what the feminists say, are necessary. Boys need a man to emulate and girls need a daddy just as much. Feminists have said many obvious untruths to the harm of women and the detriment of society as a whole. Some of these statements are absurd and obviously untrue, such as there is no difference between boys and girls except for the difference imposed upon them by our culture. Men and woman are not just anatomically different, we think differently and experience emotions in different ways. It is not a matter of better or worse, but different. These differences, if under God, glorify God and enrich both men and women. Abortion and birth control are about preventing men from becoming fathers and the human species from perpetuating itself. Also the effect of birth control is we have men and women pleasuring themselves, shunning the consequences and obligations that must accompany sexual intimacy. This is displeasing to the Lord. This is rebellion and it brings a curse on the land especially with the shedding of innocent blood. Abortion is blood sacrifice to wanton sexuality. This is a spiritual issue. The issues here are the nature of Man, the nature of God and living a life that is aligned to the will of God. Even in the Old Testament it says of the Lord, "Did he not make them one, having a remnant of the Spirit? And why one? He seeks godly offspring ["seed" in the King James Version]. Therefore take heed to your spirit, and let none deal treacherously with the wife of his youth" (Malachi 2:15, NKJV).

Despite what many radicals say, fatherhood is important and families do need fathers. Jesus said that earthly fathers may learn from and apply principles of fatherhood from their heavenly Father (Matthew 7:7-12). John the Baptist preached that although earthly fathers are important, it is far more important to have a spiritual renewal and transformation of the heart and thereby come to know God as Father (Matthew 3:9). It doesn't matter if you are a Jew or an Arab, black or white, male or female. What matters is being fathered into the Kingdom of God through Jesus by the power of the Holy Spirit.

The Assyrians
The Last Aramaic Speakers

Before 2003, Iraq's Christian population was estimated to be around 5% of the total population. Due to Islamist/Jihadist insurgents targeting Iraq's Christian minority with violent attacks, many Iraqi Christians have become refugees and several thousands have fled Iraq. Two important groups of Iraqi Christians are the Assyrians and the Chaldeans. Both Assyrians and Chaldeans speak Modern Neo-Aramaic, a modern form of the ancient Aramaic language. Aramaic was the language that was spoken by Jesus Christ according to several references from the New Testament. Before the insurgency, there were over 200,000 Assyrians and over 800,000 Chaldeans in Iraq. There is also an Assyrian community in Iran. Assyrians in Iran live along the coast of Lake Urmiyah and also in the city of Tehran.

The Assyrian Language:

The Assyrians speak Modern Assyrian Neo-Aramaic. Aramaic is a Semitic language that is closely related to Hebrew and Arabic. During church services, both Assyrians and Chaldeans use Syriac as a liturgical language. (Syriac is an ancient form of Aramaic that was spoken in the city of Edessa. It is very similar to the Aramaic that was spoken by Jesus of Nazareth.) Sometimes, Modern

Assyrian Aramaic is called Modern Syriac. However, this is incorrect as there are no immediate descendants of Syriac spoken today. Syriac is an ancient form of Aramaic and is more similar to the Aramaic Christ spoke than modern Aramaic is. There are scattered pockets of Aramaic-speaking Christian communities in Syria, Turkey, Iraq and Iran. The Maronites in Lebanon and the Saint Thomas Christians in India also use Syriac as a liturgical/theological language. There are different dialects of modern Aramaic. Assyrians and Chaldeans actually speak different dialects. They are mutually intelligible, however, Assyrians can better understand the Chaldean dialect than Chaldeans can understand Assyrians. Assyrians are more likely to be able to read and write in Aramaic than are Chaldeans. While many Chaldeans speak Neo-Aramaic, many do not and on average Chaldeans are much further along on the path of "Arabization" (complete assimilation into Arab culture) than are the Assyrians.

The Titles "Assyrian" and "Chaldean"

There is a considerable amount of controversy over the titles "Assyrian" and "Chaldean" among these respective groups. They are very passionate about these titles and can become deeply offended by what they perceive as a misuse of these terms. The ecclesiastical background of those who call themselves "Assyrian" is the Church of the East.

The Chaldeans are descendants of Christians who were from the Church of the East but joined themselves to the Roman Catholic Church. Assyrians do not recognize that the Chaldeans are truly Chaldeans. Assyrians take great pride in their ethnicity. From their point of view, the "Chaldeans" are a group of Assyrians that converted to the Roman Catholic Church. The Chaldeans do not recognizes the term "Assyrian" as legitimate and look upon people they view as "Assyrian nationalists" with contempt. Assyrians view themselves as the direct descendants of the ancient Assyrians of the Assyrian Empire. They are very serious about this and take great pride in their ancestral heritage. The Chaldeans view themselves as the descendents of the ancient Chaldeans and Babylonians and see themselves as the heirs of the mighty ancient Babylonian Empire and take great pride in their history as Babylonians.

Assyrian Beginnings

Every February, Assyrians celebrate a holiday called "the Rogation of the Ninevites" in which they remember the repentance of their ancient Assyrian ancestors at the preaching of the prophet Jonah as is recorded in the Old Testament. According to accounts written by the early church fathers, Mesopotamian Christianity was established by the Apostles Saint Thomas ("doubting Thomas") and the Apostle Thaddeus. The account is that Saint

Thaddeus and Saint Mari preached to King Abgar of Edessa and then traveled throughout Mesopotamia preaching the Gospel. The Assyrians use the Divine Liturgy of Mari and Thaddeus, which is one of the oldest liturgies than is currently in use in the world. Many important early church fathers and theologians composed important theological and historical books in the Syriac language.

The Apostles of the Assyrian Church

The Gospel of Matthew declares that the fame of Christ spread throughout all of Syria—meaning Aramaic speaking areas—during his ministry (Matthew 4:24). Two apostles carried the Gospel to the East, Thaddeus and Thomas. (Paul may also have preached to Aramaic speaking people first. It is possible that when Paul went to Arabia that he went to the Nabatean Empire of Petra in Jordan and preached to the Aramaic speaking Arabs under King Aretas. King Aretas was probably trying to arrest Paul for his efforts at converting his fellow Aramaic speakers to faith in Jesus. See Galatians 1:17 and 1 Corinthians 11: 32-3. When Paul says he is a "Hebrew of the Hebrews" in Philippians 3:5 he means that he was raised an Aramaic speaking religious Jew. Both Tarsus, where Paul was from, and Damascus, where Paul became a Christian, were Aramaic speaking cities.) One of the reasons we know that Aramaic was the language of Jesus is because he gave his disciples Aramaic names, or they had Aramaic names already. Simon the Son of Jonah was given the Aramaic nick-name Cephas, meaning 'Stone'. James and John were nick-named Boanerges, Aramaic for "Sons of Thunder." Judah was given the Aramaic nick-name Thomas, meaning 'Twin'perhaps because of his close physical resemblance to Jesus. The other Simon was called Simon the Terrorist. In Aramaic it is Canaanean and is usually translated as Simon the Zealot. Zealots used violent means to oppose Roman occupation. Jesus was willing to accept people with shameful pasts if they were willing to follow him. Magdala in the name Mary Magdalene means "Tower". Saint Jerome suggested Christ gave her this name because her faith was as a tower. Martha is Aramaic for 'Lady'. Judas Thaddeus has a very interesting name. Simon as a Zealot was a man who had been a man of anger prone to violence. But Judas' Aramaic name shows him to be a very tender and loving man. In Aramaic Thaddeus means "breast". In Aramaic there is also a connection to the word for nipple. This Judas, not Iscariot, also had another name besides that of Thaddeus. It is Lebbaeus. This is the Aramaic word for heart. Thaddeus Lebbaeus means "breast" and "heart". Thaddeus was obviously "all heart". He was a tender and sensitive man who loved people. It was this meek and loving man who converted the Assyrian Kingdom to faith in Jesus. This man of love is the father of the

Aramaic church. In Modern Aramaic Thaddeus is called Addai. (Judas Thaddeus called Lebbaus is mentioned in Matthew 10:4 and Mark 3:18. Thaddeus was numbered among the Seventy disciples of Jesus whose mission is described in Luke 10:1-24.)

Eusebius Pamphylius, the father of church history, wrote of the conversion of Abgar the king of the Aramaic peoples in his *Ecclesiastical History* which was written around 325 A.D. According to this tradition Abgar, who was ailing, heard of the miraculous power of Jesus and sent a letter to him requesting that he visit and heal him, Jesus responded that after his glorification he would send a disciple to minister unto him. After Pentecost, Saint Thomas sent Thaddeus and the disciple Mari to preach to King Abgar. Thaddeus prayed for Abgar and Abgar was immediately miraculously healed. Thaddeus baptized King Abgar into the church. After seeing the miracles and listening to the gentle wisdom of a kind and caring man that Thaddeus was many of the Aramaic speakers and the Assyrians also were converted. Eusebius, called the Father of Church History, writing in 325 says he found the records of the Apostles ministry to the Assyrians written in Aramaic among the official records of the city of Edessa. Eusebius translated these documents in the archives from the original Aramaic. This letter reads as follows

Abgarus, King of Edessa, to Jesus the good Savior, who appears at Jerusalem, greeting. I have been informed concerning you and your cures, which are performed without the use of medicines and herbs. For it is reported, that you cause the blind to see, the lame to walk, do both cleanse lepers, and cast out unclean spirits and devils and restore to health who have been long diseased, and raiseth up the dead; all which I heard, I was persuaded one of these two: wither that you are God himself descended form heaven, who do these things, or the son of God. On this account therefore I have wrote unto you, earnestly to desire that you would take the trouble of a journey hither, and cure a disease which I am under. For I hear the Judeans ridicule you, and intend you mischief. My city is indeed small, but neat, and large enough for us both.

Jesus verbally responded,

Abgarus, you are happy, for as much as you have believed on me, whom ye have not seen. For it is written concerning me, that those who have seen me should not believe on me, that they who have not seen might believe and live. As to that part of your letter, which relates to my giving you a visit, I must inform you, that I must fulfill all the ends of my mission in this country, and after that be received up again to him who sent me. But after my ascension I will send one of my disciples, who will cure your disease, and give life to you, and all that are with you.

Thomas also ministered to the Assyrians and went on to preach in India. *The Doctrine of Addai* is an Aramaic work describing the ministry of Thaddeus and other of the apostles to the Aramaic peoples. *The Acts of Thomas*, also written in Aramaic, describes the ministry of Thomas in India. *The Doctrine of Addai* not only tells the amazing and fascinating story of Thaddeus and the founding of the Assyrian Church it also introduces the core principles of Christianity. This book is written to introduce Christian doctrine in a way that is easy to understand for the layman. Thaddeus the Heart loved people and he wanted them to understand the Good News of Jesus in a simple way. This important theological work of Thaddeus has been preserved for us in the original Aramaic by the Assyrian nation. The Diving liturgy used by Assyrian Christians called "The Hallowing of the

Holy Apostles Mar Mani and Mar Addai" is also believed to have been composed by Thaddeus. It has been determined to be the oldest liturgy still in use in the world. This liturgy is still recited in the ancient Aramaic language of Jesus. Ian Wilson believes that St. Thomas, Thaddeus and Mari brought the shroud of Jesus and gave it as a gift to Abgar. This shroud, Wilson has determined, was stolen from the Assyrians by western Christians, and eventually found its way to Turin Italy where it is preserved today.

Jesus gave his disciples a commission to go forth into the entire world with his divine message. Christians often focus on the deeds of St. Paul and St. Peter and the apostles who ministered in the west while they overlook the endeavors of St. Thomas and Saint Thaddeus and other apostles who preached the Good News to the east. This is the story of the conversion of the Assyrians. The Assyrians are still with us today and they still speak the language of Jesus, Aramaic, as their native tongue. This version of *The Doctrine of Addai* is based on the ancient historical references and old Aramaic manuscripts. It tells of the beginning of the Aramaic church in Mesopotamia. The church that Jesus founded and that had its headquarters in Jerusalem was of course an Aramaic church. *The Doctrine of Addai* tells the story of how the Jews, Israelites and Assyrians of Assyria, Babylonia and Chaldea first heart the message of Jesus the Messiah from his holy apostles Saint Thomas, Saint Thaddeus and Saint Mari. (*The Doctrine of Addai* is called *Mallepanuta d-Addai Shelikha* in Aramaic.)

The Assyrian Church:

The Assyrian Church has been called the Nestorian Church in the past. Assyrians even called themselves Nestorians until fairly recently. The proper name for this church is "the Church of the East." Nestorius (circa 386-circa 451 A.D.) was a Patriarch of Constantinople who was deposed and condemned as a heretic for teaching that Jesus Christ had two separate natures, a human nature and a divine nature. This led to considerable controversy in the early church. Eventually, the church declared that Christ has two natures but they are united. This controversy split the church into several factions, Nestorians, Monophysites and the orthodox Roman Catholic and Greek Orthodox. (The Monophysites deny Christ has two natures. They teach that he has one divine nature. The Coptic, Ethiopic, Syrian Orthodox and Armenian Church are Monophysite. They now seem to be objecting to the term "Monophysites" and prefer to be referred to as Henophysites.) These old Christological controversies may seem very arcane and irrelevant, but they are very important to Eastern Christians and are very important to understand when relating to Eastern Christians, especially for clergy.) The Assyrian Church of the

East is Trinitarian and the Nicene Creed is recited during Holy Communion. In the course of ecumenical dialogue, the Roman Catholic Church has declared that it no longer views the Church of the East as heretical. The term "Nestorian" could possibly be viewed as pejorative or derogatory and should be avoided when speaking to Assyrians. (It may be helpful when writing books and articles when referring to the Church of the East to note for clarification that it was known as the Nestorian Church. But this title is no longer proper terminology.) Some Assyrians object to being called "Nestorian" for the following reasons. First, Nestorius didn't found their Church, the Holy Apostles did hundreds of years before Nestorius. Secondly, although they did accept "Nestorian" theologians, neither they nor Nestorius, ever taught the "Nestorian" heresy (the heresy that Jesus Christ is composed of two *persons*-the human and the divine).

The Church of the East

The Church of the East was once widespread throughout Asia. Archeologists have found remains of Assyrian church buildings in China and all across central Asia. Assyrian Christian literature has been found in the Chinese language hidden in caves in China. A monument dated to the year 781 tells of how in the year 636 the Chinese Emperor granted permission for Assyrian Christians to build churches, translate the Bible into Chinese and preach Christianity in the Chinese Empire. This monument is written in Chinese and Syriac. Marco Polo mentions seeing "Nestorian" churches all across his travels. Although the Church of the East was spread from Baghdad all the way to Beijing due to plague and long and sustained religious persecution from Muslim warlords, the Church of the East declined and dwindled into a small community in northern Iraq and Western Iran with a few churches in Western India.

The International Assyrian Community

Assyrians consider northern Iraq, called *Beth Nahrain* in Aramaic, as their homeland. There is a large and important Assyrian community in Urmiyah and Tehran in Iran. Many Assyrians fleeing from ethnic cleansing in Iraq during the 1930s have settled in the Khabur River Valley region of eastern Syria. Assyrians have been immigrating to the west for over one hundred years. There are large Assyrian American communities in Chicago, Illinois and Turlock and Modesto California. (Chaldeans have immigrated to San Diego, California and the Detroit area of Michigan.) Australia also has a large Assyrian community. Many Aramaic –speakers (some Assyrian but mostly Suryoyo-speaking Syrian Orthodox) have immigrated to Sweden. These communities support their fellow Assyrians in the Middle East. There are several Assyrian organizations and societies such as "the Assyrian Aide Society" and "the Assyrian Democratic Movement" which is a political party in Iraq. (There are also many Assyrian publications, websites and even musical albums.)

Assyrian Christian Groups

The leader of the Assyrian Church is the Catholicos-Patriarch. Originally, the Patriarch was elected by bishops. During a long period of intense persecution by Muslim rulers, the practice of passing the office from patriarch to his nephew began. This led to inadequate leadership. The position of Patriarch was religious and political. As non-Muslims, Assyrians were Dhimmis ("people of the book" which means a group that is tolerated but denied equal rights by the Islamic community). The Patriarch was the recognized leader of this particular group of dhimmis by the Muslims rulers. This hereditary system resulted in the Chaldean schism, led in 1553 by John Sulaqa. A previous Church of the East Patriarch was Mar Shimon XXIII who was assassinated by an Assyrian in San Jose, California in November 1975 after he had retired from office and married. (Assyrians still remember the murder of Mar Shimon XXI by a Kurdish chieftain in 1918 but seem to be embarrassed by the fact than an Assyrian murdered the Patriarch and while I have had many encounters with Assyrians, I have never heard them talk about the murder of Mar Shimon XXIII.) The patriarch of the Church of the East Mar Dinkha IV (born 1935) has led the Assyrian community from Illinois. Mar Dinkha has made efforts to unite the Church of the East with the Roman Catholic Church. However, this led to turmoil, conflict and a lawsuit with his priest who was representing the Assyrian Church to the Roman Catholic Church. There is also an Assyrian group that calls itself the Ancient Church of the East. This faction has had its own Patriarch, Mar Addai II, and follows the old calendar. (Mar Shimun XXIII introduced the modern Gregorian Calendar but the Ancient Church of the East prefers the older Julian Calendar. Mar Addai II resided in Baghdad.) There are also Assyrian Protestants. Many Assyrian Protestants belong to the Presbyterian Church due to the fact that Presbyterians came to Iran during the 1800s to work with the Assyrians.

Religious persecution

Islam is a religion and a political system. Moslems are members of the *umma,* which can be translated as "the nation" or "the community." Although Assyrians are the indigenous people of Iraq, they are viewed as "outsiders" by many Moslems, since they, as non-Muslims, are outside the *umma.* As non-Muslims they are often discriminated against. During the Armenian Genocide of 1914-1915, 1.5 million Armenians were killed by Turks and tens of thousands of Assyrians were also slaughtered. Throughout the nineteenth and early twentieth centuries Kurds and Turks carried out several pogroms and massacres of Assyrian Christians. The Assyrians volunteered to fight for the British during both World War I and World War II, hoping that the British would protect them from religious persecution. The Assyrians fought in a decisive conflict against Nazis in Iraq at Fallujah during World War II and were instrumental in achieving a major victory there. The Assyrians feel they were betrayed by the British and feel the British are partly to blame for the pogroms and ethnic cleansing that occurred after World War I and World War II. (Some Assyrians feel that an independent Assyrian nation should have been created after World War I.) Assyrians endured ethnic and religious persecution under the regime of Saddam Hussein (but also had a certain level of protection from religious violence). After the fall of Saddam Hussein insurgents have targeted Assyrians for terrorist attacks and have bombed churches during religious services and have assassinated clergy. With the surge some stability has returned. The Assyrians face an uncertain future in Iraq.

Resources with Additional Information:
Internet: The Assyrian International News Agency
www.aina.org, www.nestorians.org ,
www.bethmardutho.org, www.nineveh.com,
Assyrian Academic Studies www.jaas.org

Books:

Samuel Hugh Moffett **A History of Christianity in Asia: Volume 1: Beginnings to 1500** (Harper San Francisco 1992) Hans-Joachim Klimkeit and Ian Gillman **Christianity in Asia Before 1500** (University of Michigan Press, 1999) Sebastian Brock **The Hidden Pearl** (Transworld Films, Italy 2001) Christoph Baumer **The Church of the East: An Illustrated History of Assyrian Christianity** (I.B. Tauris, June 2006)

An Aramaic Resource Guide

TO LEARN MORE ABOUT Aramaic as the language of Jesus: Many great Bible scholars have done research on the Aramaic source of Christ's teachings. This includes Joachim Jeremias, Bruce Chilton, Maurice Casey, Martin McNamara, Matthew Black, Gustav Dalman and others. George Mamishisho Lama was an Assyrian American who wrote many very interesting and easy to read commentaries on the New Testament from the Aramaic perspective.

Aramaic Versions of the New Testament

There are several English translations of the New Testament from the Aramaic version, most notably the translation by John Wesley Etheridge. Gorgias Press has the translation from the Syriac by James Murdock available. James Murdock, trans. *The New Testament Translated from the Peshitto Version* (Gorgias Press, New Jersey 2001). Gorgias Press has many books on the Syriac Christian heritage available. They also have a video available entitled *The Last Assyrians.*

Joseph Paskha has translated *The Aramaic Gospel and Acts* and has written a key to aide in the pronunciation of the Aramaic. An Interlinear Aramaic New Testament is freely available at www.peshitta.org. George Mamishishu Lamsa, Vic Alexander and Jan Magiera have all translated the New Testament from Aramaic into English.

Aramaic Sources to the New Testament

Maurice Casey has written two helpful Aramaic books *Aramaic Sources of Mark's_Gospel* and *An Aramaic Approach to Q: Sources for the Gospels of Matthew and Luke*. These books are published by Cambridge University Press. His chapters of the languages spoken in the Holy Land at the time of Christ are excellent. Also, he uses only Aramaic from the Holy Land that has been dated to the time of Christ to reconstruct the words of Jesus in the original Aramaic.

Joachim Jeremais lived from 1900 until 1979 in Germany. Helpful books by Joachim Jeremias include, *The Basic Message of the New Testament*, *New Testament Theology*, and *The Prayers of Jesus*. Joachim Jeremias is one of the best and most respected experts on Aramaic and the life of Christ who lived in the twentieth century.

The Poetry of Our Lord: An Examination of the Formal Elements of Hebrew Poetry in the Discourses of Jesus Christ by Rev. C.F. Burney in 1925 is useful. He also wrote a book on the Aramaic Origin of the Fourth Gospel.

Charles Cutler Torrey also wrote about Aramaic and the New Testament in *Our Translated Gospels: Some of the Evidence.*

One of the best examinations of the words of Jesus in the Aramaic is *The Words of Jesus: Considered in the Light of Post-Biblical Jewish Writings and the Aramaic Language* by Gustav Dalman and *An Aramaic Approach to the Gospels and Acts* by Matthew Black.

Mel Gibson's *The Passion of the Christ Definitive Edition* DVD contains two versions of the "Passion of the Christ" movie and also a documentary on Aramaic by Mel Gibson's Aramaic authority, Father William Fulco.

The Targums

Martin McNamara *Targum and Testament: Aramaic Paraphrases of the Hebrew Bible: A Light on the New Testament.*
John Ronning has written *The Jewish Targums and John's Logos Theology* in which he illuminates the stunning ways the Aramaic tradition gives revelation into the meaning of John's "Logos Theology."
Bruce Chilton is the author of *A Galilean Rabbi and His Bible* and *Rabbi Jesus: An Intimate Biography*

both of which use the Aramaic Targums to understand the teachings of Christ.

A. Sperber has composed *The Bible in Aramaic: Based on Old Manuscripts and Printed Texts.* A multi-volume annotated translation of the Aramaic Targum into English is also available. In this edition, each book of the Bible is printed and bound separately, such as "The Targum of Jeremiah," "The Targum of Ezekiel" and etcetera. This series of books is published by the Liturgical Press and is entitled *The Aramaic Bible: The Targums.*

Israel Drazin, a former military chaplain, has written extensively on the Aramaic Targums including in his book *Onkelos on the Torah: Understanding the Bible Text.*

The Aramaic Christian Heritage

Samuel Hugh Moffett *A History of Christianity in Asia Volume I: Beginnings to 1500* (Harper San Francisco 1992)

Hans-Joachim Klimkeit and Ian Gillman *Christians in Asia Before 1500* (University of Michigan Press 1999)

Sebastian P. Brock and Davis G. K. Taylor *The Hidden Pearl: The Syrian Orthodox Church and Its Ancient Aramaic Heritage: Volume I The Ancient Aramaic Heritage Volume II the Heirs of the*

Ancient Aramaic Heritage Volume III At the Turn of the Third Millennium, the Syrian Orthodox Witness (Transworld Films, Italy 2001) with accompanying videotapes.

Christoph Baumer *The Church of the East: An Illustrated History of Assyrian Christianity.*

The Lost Sutras of Jesus: Unlocking the Ancient Wisdom of the Xian Monks by Ray Riegent. Martin Palmer *The Jesus Sutras: Rediscovering the Lost Scrolls of Taoist Christianity* (Ballantine Wellspring, New York 2001)

Beth Mardutho www.bethmardutho.org and www.nestorian.org are helpful websites on the Assyrian Church of the East (as well as the Syrian Orthodox Church and other Syriac Christian Churches) as well as the Nestorian Pages, or 'Syriac Christianity in Central Asia by Mark Dickens' at www.oxuscom.com

The Assyrian Christians

Rev. John Booko has written *The Assyrian Revelation* and *Assyria: The Forgotten Nation in Biblical Prophecy.*

The Assyrians: The Continuous Saga by Frederick A. Aprim (Xlibris Corporation, 2004)

Moranetho: The Assyrian Church of the East in the Twentieth Century by Mar Aprem published in India is a helpful history of the modern era of the Assyrian Church.

The Flickering Light of Asia, or the Assyrian Nation and Church written by Rev. Joel Werda in 1924.

The Untold Holocaust is a documentary about genocidal attacks against Aramaic Christians by Muslims and massacres of Aramaic Christians by Muslims that features interviews with some of the survivors, by Australian Assyrian Academic Society

Journal of Assyrian Academic Studies is a scholarly journal that focuses on the history of Assyrian Christians (www.jaas.org).

Aramaic Jews

Ariel Sabar wrote of his father Yona and of his Aramaic heritage in *My Father's Paradise: A Son's Search for His Jewish Past in Kurdish Iraq*.

There are many Assyrian bands that play Aramaic traditional music, church music and even Aramaic Rock-n-roll. There is a Jewish Aramaic music band called Nash Didan that does traditional and contemporary Aramaic music.

Learning Aramaic

A good Biblical Aramaic grammar and workbook for beginners is Frederick E. Greenspahn's *An Introduction to Aramaic* (Scholars Press, Atlanta Georgia 1999).

The best tool to learn Aramaic online is currently Alan Al-Dawood's "Teach Yourself Aramaic" www.assyrianlanguge.com. There is also Robert Oshana's "Learn Assyrian Online" www.learnassyrian.com.

"Teach Yourself Modern Syriac" is a very helpful CD-ROM available from Esarhaddon Productions.

W. M. Thackston's *Introduction to Syriac* is a good introduction to the Classical Aramaic used in Church services by Assyrian Christians.

Father Michael J. Bazzi, a Chaldean Catholic priest and native Aramaic speaker has written a very helpful *Beginner's Handbook of the Aramaic Chaldean Alphabets.*

Understanding Islam

Aramaic people have had to live under the dominion of Islam for over 1,000 years. For this reason, I believe that people interested in Aramaic Christianity need to have a proper understanding of

Islam. This is very difficult due to the amount of disinformation coming from political correctness (which in turn comes from Academia and the Liberal News Media) and the influence of Saudi Arabian Petrol-dollars. For accurate information I recommend the following books: Serge Trikovic, *The Sword of the Prophet: Islam, history, theology, impact on the world*, Aramaic Christian Brigitte Gabriel, *Because they Hate: A Survivor of Islamic Terror Warns America* and *They Must Be Stopped*, Nonie Darwish, *Now They Call Me Infidel: Why I renounced Jihad for America, Israel, and the War on Terror* and Walid Shoebat *Why I Left Jihad* and *Why We Want to Kill You*. Most of these books I recommend here are written by Arabs and Arabic Christians. These people have grown up in an Islamic culture and thus they know what they are talking about and are very blunt. I also recommend books on Islam written by Robert Spencer. I also recommend two documentaries *Islam: What the West Needs to Know* and *Obsession: Radical Islam's War Against the West*. Helpful websites include www.thereligionofpeace.com, www.thetruthofislam.com and www.campus-watch.org. It is also important to have a proper understanding of the Crusades. I strongly recommend *God's Battalions* by Rodney Stark. I also believe educated people needs to have an understanding of what the Koran really says and teaches. For this reason I recommend *An Abridged*

Koran: Readable and Understandable by the Center for the Study of Political Islam.

Helpful Web-sites

Current information on the Assyrians can be found at Nineveh Online www.nineveh.com, Zinda Magazine www.zindamagazine.com and Assyrian International New Agency www.aina.org

Aramaic Bible Translation sells Bible movies, including the "Jesus" film, in the Aramaic language and also has audio Bibles. (The Jesus film is a two-hour film based on the account of the life of Christ found in the Gospel of Luke. The "Jesus Video Project" is an attempt to dub this film into every language on earth, including modern dialects of Aramaic.) They are currently located at 100 Wycliffe Drive, West Chicago, Illinois, 60185. Visit them online at www.aramaicbible.org or call 630-876-8452. A dramatic presentation of the Gospel of John in Modern Aramaic is also available.

The San Antonio Vocal Arts Ensemble (SAVAE) has put together a beautiful collection of Aramaic music entitled *Ancient Echoes.*

The Barnabas Fund gives aide to persecuted Aramaic Christians in the Near East. Barnabas Fund, 6731 Curran St., McLean, VA 22101. The

Barnabas fund is online at www.barnabasfund.org and can also be reached by phone at (703) 288-1681, toll-free 1-866-936-2525 or can be reached via email at bfusa@barnabasfund.org.

BOOKS BY THE AUTHOR

The Words of Jesus in the Original Aramaic:
Discovering the Semitic Roots of Christianity

Mary of Magdala: Magdalene, the Forgotten
Aramaic Prophetess of Christianity

Treasures of the Language of Jesus: The Aramaic
Source of Christ's Teaching

Aramaic: The Language of Jesus of Nazareth

Christ the Man

The Hammer of God: The Stories of Judah
Maccabee and Charles Martel

The Ascents of James: A Lost Acts of the Apostles

The Second Adam and the Restoration of All Things

Comic Books:

The Assyrians: The Oldest Christian People
Chronicles: Facts from the Bible
The Hammer of God: Character and Historical
Reference
The Hammer of God Coloring Book
The Hammer of God Mini-Comic

About the Author

Reverend Stephen Andrew Missick is the author of *The Assyrian Church in the Mongol Empire*, *Mar Thoma: The Apostolic Foundation of the Assyrian Church in India*, and *Socotra: The Mysterious Island of the Church of the East* which were published in the Journal of Assyrian Academic Studies (Volume XIII, No. 2, 1999, Volume XIV, No. 2, 2000 and Volume XVI No. 1, 2002). He is the author of *The Words of Jesus in the Original Aramaic: Discovering the Semitic Roots of Christianity*, *Mary of Magdala: Magdalene, the Forgotten Aramaic Prophetess of Christianity*, *Treasures of the Language of Jesus: The Aramaic Source of Christ's Teaching*, *Aramaic: The Language of Jesus of Nazareth* and *Christ the Man*. He is an ordained minister of the gospel. He graduated from Sam Houston State University and Southwestern Baptist Theological Seminary. Rev. Missick has traveled extensively throughout the Middle East and has lived among the Coptic Christians in Egypt and Aramaic Christians in Syria. He also served as a soldier in Operation Iraqi Freedom in 2003 and 2004. While serving as a soldier in Iraq he learned Aramaic from native Aramaic-speaking Iraqi Assyrian Christians. Rev. Missick is the writer and illustrator of the comic book "The Assyrians: The Oldest Christian People," the comic strip *Chronicles: Facts from the Bible* and the comic book series *The Hammer of God* which are available from www.comixpress.com. *The Hammer of God* comic book series dramatizes the stories of Judah Maccabee and Charles Martel. He has also served as a chaplain in the Army National Guard in Iraq during his second deployment in 2009 and 2010.

Contact Stephen A. Missick at PO Box 882 Shepherd TX 77371 A monthly newsletter, *The Aramaic Herald*, is available free of charge. DVDs and Gospel tracts with an Aramaic focus are also available from the above address. Rev. Missick has several short video teachings and presentations at www.youtube.com/aramaic12 and a blog at www.aramaicherald.blogspot.com.

Made in the USA
Columbia, SC
04 August 2022

64552879R00068